TABOON

TABOON

— A traditional Palestinian portable oven made from clay and straw.

— A soft, pillowy, dimpled flatbread cooked in a taboon oven. Local names and cooking methods for the bread differ from place to place, but it is a staple across the region.

HISHAM ASSAAD

SWEET & SAVOURY DELIGHTS
FROM THE LEBANESE BAKERY

TABOON

Smith
Street
Books

Contents

06
INTRODUCTION

18
Breads & Topped Breads

60
Savoury Snacks

98
Bakery Sweets

128
Cookies & Cakes

164
Sweets & Desserts

202
INDEX

206
ACKNOWLEDGEMENTS

Introduction

"You are now family. There will be bread and salt between us."

This is a common and ancient saying in Arabic on welcoming someone into a household – reflecting that the sharing of basic commodities like bread and salt is the basis of friendship and trust. These have always been symbols of hospitality, and although the practice of sharing bread and salt is no longer observed, the people of Bilad al Sham – the Levant – still get together around food. Whenever we're meeting someone, we'll always have a table full of food. Weddings, funerals, memorials, all have their traditional foods – no matter the occasion, we will make sure to give everyone a good meal. It has always been this way, no matter how hard the times. So grab a piece of bread and a sprinkle of salt and join me in the place where I grew up.

The bakeries

Everywhere in Lebanon, or wherever you go across the region, you will find a small bakery that makes a great *manouche*, the singular of *manakish*. Whether these topped breads are made in a regular gas oven or a wood-fired one, in a *tannour*, a *taboon*, or on a *saj*, it is very hard to go wrong with such a basic delicacy. But bakeries here aren't just about *manakish*, from French baguettes to sourdough loaves – our want and need for bread is wider than ever. Some specialise in making sesame-crusted *kaaké* (or *ka'ak*) breads, which are plate-sized flatbread parcels filled with olive oil and za'atar or sumac or a mix of cheeses; or small rolls to be filled with sweet cheese-rich *Knefe* (page 121). Some make *kaak* – crunchy breadsticks covered in sesame, sometimes flavoured with za'atar or other spices. The plain sesame ones are excellent dipped into tea.

Different types of bread come in and out of popularity. Years ago, *Saj* bread (also called *marqouq*, page 26) was not commonly available, as few bakeries made it. But now we love it because it's a versatile, thin bread, good for scooping or using in wraps. *Saj manouche* are thinner and crunchier too.

It used to be common, and still is in some parts of the city and in villages, to take your own toppings to bakeries to make your own *manouche*. On certain Saturdays, my mom would take a tray full of containers of toppings she had prepared to the bakery in the next street: za'atar mixed with olive oil; shredded Akkawi cheese, rinsed very well to remove its saltiness; chilli and onion paste; labneh with tomatoes and green onions. She would wait in line to make the pies herself. The baker would take the already portioned and rested dough balls, pass them through a rolling machine to the desired thickness and lay them out on a wooden plank to rest further before passing them to my mom to generously spread with the toppings. They would be deftly slid, one by one, into the oven and would bake in a few minutes. I would help her fold each one in half when they came out of the oven and would carry the large tray of *manakish* home, ready for breakfast with vegetables, olives and black tea.

Sweet shops

During the month of Ramadan, shops put out displays of their specialty sweets, breads and classical desserts. The windows are full of *atayef* (pancakes filled with *ashta/* clotted cream or walnuts), tray-baked *maamoul* with *ashta*, and *hadef baklawa* (walnut baklava), *mafrouke* (page 126), *meshtah* (page 28) and the most sought-after *kallaj* (see page 192) that is usually freshly made in the 30 minutes before *iftar* (breaking fast), which makes shops significantly more crowded at that time. Although most of these items are available year-round, eating them at this time of year has a more special significance.

I've visited Tripoli and Saida during Ramadan, and the streets after *iftar* time are bustling with life, a drastic change from the calmer days, with live performances in some squares and tables set up outside shops to sell and serve food. In Saida I've had huge cheese *atayef*, which is similar in concept to the kataifi pastry coated *Knefe* (page 121), but made with soft *atayef* dough that is stuffed with rinsed Akkawi cheese and served with syrup. And that's far from the only thing you might try in Saida: *Shaabiyat* (page 110), *Maamoul* (page 132) and the well known *Ghraybe* (page 143) are all worth seeking out. In Tripoli you might try *Arayes* (page 88) and some *Ma'arouk* (page 142), but you can't miss *Halawet el Jeben* (page 124) and *Halawet el Shmayse* (page 122).

In my trips around the souks, I was able to get a few of the trade secrets from chatting to and befriending the makers of all those delicious sweets. It was important for me to find the right ways, and the most authentic ways, of making and preserving these recipes. I've improvised a little too, where I found an opportunity to do so and it wouldn't completely destroy the original recipe.

My family history

In my first book, I didn't delve very deeply into my family roots and history. I barely scratched the surface. But I'm proud of my heritage, and since we're family now – we've broken bread and salt – I want to tell you more about them.

I am the grandson of Palestinians who were expelled from their village during Al Nakba ("the catastrophe") in 1948, which, under British mandate, gave Palestinian lands to Jewish settlers to build the nation of Israel. That act, the 50 years preceding, and the time leading up to this day, were nothing short of traumatic. My family moved from their village Al-Bassa, near the south Lebanon border (now a settlement called Shlomi), which had taken its independence from the French mandate only five years before Al Nakba, to the safety of Lebanon until the time they could return to their homes. Believing they could return, they left with their house keys and barely any belongings. From the south of Lebanon, they were moved to live in tents in an area between Tyre and Sidon (an area which is still a large refugee camp), but were then asked to move to other areas to set up their camps. Most Christians lived in Mar Elias, Jisr El Bacha and in Dbayeh, which is where my family settled.

The Dbayeh refugee camp was established in 1952 on the side of a hill overlooking the Mediterranean Sea, 12 km (7.5 mi) from Beirut and towered over by the Maronite monastery of Saint Joseph. It housed families in tents before they built walls for more secure living, when months later they realised their return would take longer. After a while, they built roofs over their heads.

An old man from the camp told me that young men and women representing the then president, Camille Chamoun, went door to door in the Dbayeh camp asking people if they wished to apply (and pay) to receive Lebanese nationality. Initially it seemed like a generous act, but it is thought (unofficially) that it was done to gain a few more Christians for the next parliamentary

elections in the face of an increasing Muslim population (yes, elections are won largely based on religious sects here and not on competency). My grandparents agreed to apply and pay and we became Lebanese citizens, with slightly better privileges than those who still have UN-issued refugee IDs or Lebanese-issued travel documents.

When I was young, I wasn't told much about our Palestinian identity. My paternal grandmother was the closest blood relative I had who knew Palestine – she was born and raised there for a while. My family lived in Dbayeh and owned a butcher's shop that my grandma ran after my grandfather passed away, leaving her with nine children. All of her seven boys learned the trade and helped in the shop until the start of the Lebanese civil war, when my grandmother pushed her children to seek work abroad to prevent them from joining the armed forces. One of her sons moved to the UAE; she joined them along with other family members. They lived there for years and it's where my mom moved after marrying my dad. My two sisters and I were born in a small town in Al Ain, close to Abu Dhabi. I was raised there and have vivid memories of the school, the markets, the neighbourhood and our two-bedroom house in which my grandma and aunt lived with us.

Eventually our family had to return to Lebanon due to regulations that limited an employee's ability to support their family. My dad stayed for his job, but my mom, then in her late twenties, had to move to Lebanon with three children in her care, the youngest barely two months old. We had nothing in Lebanon, but relatives offered support us until we were established. It was not easy. To be a young mother with three children in a country she didn't remember much of and with my dad working abroad, it was definitely a challenge. I give my mom all credit for taking up that responsibility and excelling at it. I wouldn't be where I am today if it wasn't for her.

I had to get used to the camp. In the UAE we were not rich by any means, but we lived in our own rented house and went to a good affordable private school (public schools were only for the locals). In my eyes as a child, this was enough. Moving into a one-room house in Dbayeh, below ground level, with barely any sunlight getting in, was a big change. The neighbourhood was different, the power would cut off, the water was inconsistent, we heard stories about crimes nearby. People spoke differently and I was mocked by other children for my mixed accent. As a young boy, this was a pivotal moment for me as I tried to fit in. It sparked an interest in finding out why we spoke differently to others, why we lived in an area called "the camp", and what had happened to make Lebanon so unstable and potentially dangerous.

Once I found out about our Palestinian identity, I asked my grandmother about Palestine. Her answers were always brief and real. She didn't paint a utopian image of Palestine. She told me about the olive groves her father owned, about how they used to harvest the olives as a big family and how her father would send her to sneak up on her older sisters to see if they were talking to boys behind his back. She told me about how during the long nights of winter families would gather to hand-roll dough to make vermicelli and how on those nights boys would use these activities as excuses to see their crushes, to be in the same room with them under the guise of vermicelli-making or other manual food work.

Reading more into the Palestinian presence in Lebanon and why some Lebanese people carry a lot of hostility against Palestinians, I started to understand that my grandma's terse recollections of Palestine could have been the result of trying to integrate into Lebanese culture. A lot of Christian families did, even the ones who didn't acquire Lebanese nationality. Palestinians in Lebanon were part of the civil war, some said a cause for the war, and so my grandma pushed her sons to get out of this cycle of crime and hatred to keep them safe. They wanted to identify more with their Lebanese nationality, for it would save them from unwanted aggression from those who had issues with Palestinians.

I carried that with me too. I worked in predominantly Christian areas, spoke with the right accent and didn't wear symbols that would mark me out as different. I wouldn't tell people that I lived in the camp until they knew me as a person and could judge me by my character, not because of where I came from. I lived in the camp for most of my life and only left in 2020 to work on my first book and be a little more independent.

Memories of food in Dbayeh

The camp felt like a small town to me, not too far from Beirut. It evolved from tents to concrete housing. It was not too shabby and I grew to like it. I was an active member in the church and community life there – I loved it. There was a nice sense of community. The area had everything you might need.

Nassim had a bakery and made the best *Qorban* (page 34) and the aromas of orange blossom and mastic would fill the street on Saturday nights when he was baking for the memorial after Sunday mass. There was the butcher, who was a gossiper and couldn't be trusted with a secret. There was the produce truck owner who would lay out his fresh produce in a small square and who everyone would buy from. Bachir Farah had the largest mini market and out front would be the centre of all gatherings. Across from it, Pierre Matar had a market with a depot in which you could get lost looking for toys and decorations during Christmas or Easter. There was Norma, who set up a clothes shop from a room in her house. And Issa Zourob had some cattle by the edge of the camp next to the hill. My mom used to send me to get a gallon of milk from them every Monday. Their son, my best friend Bakhomios who is now a priest, would leave the laundry or any housework he was attending to and chat with me while straining the fresh milk into our container. Mom made fresh *laban* (yoghurt) and when she didn't have any *rawbé* (a small portion of yoghurt from the previous batch needed for the fermentation), she'd send me to one of our friends or neighbours to get a coffee cup's worth to culture the milk.

On special occasions, the whole camp would fill up with scents of the foods prepared for the day. On the day before Lent and Easter Sunday (if not every Sunday), the whole street would be filled with smoke from barbecued chicken and beef. In the week before Easter, the fragrance of butter from *Maamoul* (page 132) would drift up the alleyways between the houses. On Easter Saturday everyone would take the large basins in which they had been proving the dough for *Ka'ak Asfar* (page 31) to the nearby bakery, where they would bake the batch for the holiday by appointment.

On Easter Sunday it was time for boiled and coloured eggs. Saint Barbara's Day would see the camp fill with kids in costumes, but from the kitchens would come the scent of aniseed that's been simmering with *Ameh* (page 184) and the rose-flavoured syrups for *atayef* (filled pancakes, the recipe is in my first cookbook, *Bayrut*), *Awaymet* (page 179), *Mshabbak* (page 173) and *Maakroun* (page 174). Epiphany in the camp is for fried *Zalabye* (page 45) served with labneh and for the past few years our house has been a hub for family and friends to join together to share the blessing of the occasion and to take home a ring or two of my mom's delicious *zalabye*.

I remember birthdays in Dbayeh, when the mothers would prepare or buy a few dozen small *manouche* (pages 46–55), *fatayer* (pages 81–7) and prepare a Lebanese *Fôret Noire* (page 155) with tinned fruits and powdered whipped cream. There would be jelly bowls, custard, crème caramel and other homemade confectionery. They were simple, heartwarming occasions.

Weddings, on the other hand, were an extravagant feast. When both the bride and groom were from the camp, each side would have a huge party on the Friday preceding the wedding, either in the middle of the street between houses or on the rooftop of the family house. At midnight, the groom and his party would move accompanied by a large drum and music to the bride's party and take her back to the groom's party. The celebration would continue until they could no longer stand. The food was homemade and simple – there would be dozens of pastries, such as small versions of *manouche*, *lahm baajine* (page 56), or *rqaqat* (pages 64–6), which are easy to grab and one can get away with eating a dozen before batting an eye. Alongside these would be piles of fried *kibbeh* (try my *muhammara*-stuffed *kibbeh* on page 67) and lots of *fatayer* (page 81) stuffed with foraged greens, spinach or fresh za'atar, along with some salads and sometimes meat on a grill, with plenty of drinks on the side. It was organic and fun.

On manouche

In 2023, "Al-Man'ouché" was enlisted by UNESCO as a culinary practice of intangible cultural heritage that should be protected. This topped flatbread is not only a staple of the Lebanese breakfast table and a quick breakfast on the go, but it is also so versatile that it has become a generic term for almost all baked doughs with toppings. One could argue that the *manouche* and pizza are distant relatives (or, if you really want to get a discussion going, that the former is the predecessor of the latter!). Lately, bakeries have been creating their own topping combinations that are sometimes genius but often plain weird, just for the curiosity factor.

Fatayer, *sfeeha* (page 74) and many other dough-based goods – what I would call Lebanese "pies" – also fall into the category of *manouche*. *Fatayer* is an umbrella term also – the plural of *fteere*, which means "pie". But to us it means any sealed pastry (we would include a calzone pizza in the category of *fatayer*, for instance). The most well known of these is the spinach *fatayer* (for which I gave a recipe in my first book, *Bayrut*), but any greens or vegetables can be used as a filling.

It is very hard to find a bad *manouche* in Lebanon – if you manage to find one, it should be a criminal offence! Most bakeries will have the option (for an extra charge) to order vegetables tucked inside the wrapped *manouche* or to stretch the dough and make it thinner, resulting in a crispier *manouche*. Whichever way you have it, enjoy with a pyramid carton of Bonjus juice, for the sake of nostalgia.

Some favourite bakeries

For visitors to Lebanon, here *are* a few notable bakeries that are worth taking a special trip to visit:

Ichkhanian is an Armenian bakery in Zokak El Blat that has been there since 1946 and is still run by descendants of the original family. They specialise in *lahmajun* (the Armenian version of *lahm baajine*) and ready-to-bake Armenian frozen goods, such as *souborek* (page 79) and *mante* (Armenian dumplings).

Krikor and his wife Laure run a small bakery next to their house in the mountain village of Baskinta at the foot of Mount Sannine. They are famous for their egg, *awarma* and cheese *manouche* (see page 52) and for the way Krikor serves them, on a tray with olives and fresh tomatoes. So much love is put into their products and the quality of ingredients is always superb, so anything you try there will be exceptional.

Furn El Sabaya in Amchit is an all-women bakery that is known for *qors beid* and *mwara'a* (page 117). Basically, anything that comes out from under their hands is good.

The Lebanese Bakery opened in Beirut around 2016 and has since opened branches in cities such as London, Bahrain, Cairo and Riyadh. What is striking is their use of local ingredients and combining them in *manouche* or pies not commonly found elsewhere.

Al Bacha Bakery in Tripoli is probably the only one left in the city that uses wood to fire their oven. They make nothing but pita bread and sesame-covered *ka'ak*. Across from that bakery is a butcher who fills the half-baked pita bread with a meat mix and they are then baked until the bread crisps up from the fat in the meat. These are the famous *sfeeha* from Tripoli.

Abou Khanjar in Akkar, North Lebanon, is famous for being one of the few *tannour* bakeries. A *tannour* is a deep stone fire pit, on the sides of which the dough is slapped to bake. The za'atar *manouche* made in a *tannour* is not to be missed. The *kishk* and *areesh* (seasoned cottage cheese) *fatayer* are also unique and delicious there. As if the food is not attraction enough, the view over the valley and green mountain across from the seating area is also stunning.

Keeping authentic recipes alive

Taboon is a collection of recipes from my Palestinian heritage, as well as ones from Lebanon and the surrounding regions, such as Syria. These recipes have been made in this region for decades, centuries, or even millennia. This geographic region is commonly known as Bilad Al Sham, a term dating to the seventh century. While "Sham" now refers to Damascus, which was the capital of this large piece of land, the term was coined by the people of the Hejaz (west of the Arabian Peninsula) for when they faced the rising sun: all of the lands on their right were *Al Yaman* and on the left were *Al Sham*. Throughout time, some referred to this land as Greater Syria (some still believe it is), with Lebanon only encompassing Mount Lebanon. The region underwent countless conquests and each occupier developed or took away from the local culture.

Recipes from this rich region have evolved over the years, while others have remained the same in essence, merely varying based on the availability of ingredients and advances in processing and cooking methods. It was pivotal for me to take pride in our recipes and document them in my books in the face of cultural appropriation and even the erasure of our existence, be that in the media or in real life. Some of these recipes predate borders. Some started in one city, spread through colonisation and cultural exchange and then became regional. Some are still made in only one city, or are known to be made best by a particular city.

We are now more aware of acts of cultural appropriation and erasure. The global consciousness is now geared towards enjoying world foods and embracing different cultures by highlighting their differences and similarities; celebrating foods as they are instead of softening the edges to suit untrained palates. I see people seeking out authentic Lebanese, Palestinian, Syrian and Iraqi recipes and learning to make them as close to the originals as possible. When it's a twist on a dish, or a version inspired by one, its history or origin is noted and celebrated.

I see people going back to gathering and processing edible greens from the wild. I see chefs seeking old and forgotten village recipes and presenting them on modern menus. We are finally connecting in more ways than we could have imagined through the love of life and food, and through the preservation of traditional values.

We've always been a people who love life, who want to celebrate, who want to live. We find humour in the darkest of situations, we make light of our misery to lessen its impact and seek the glimmer of light that will carry us through. We find solace in one another, in gatherings, in food, in traditions that make us feel safe and at home, no matter where we are – in tents or under solid roofs.

Writing this book was a really tough process for me and for many involved in it. The events going on in the world at the time of writing are horrific and traumatising. Across the border from me, people don't have flour to make bread, and for those who do have it, it is stained with the blood of their loved ones. The only thing that has kept me going through these times is to create. We create art even in the worst times. We create art as a time capsule for future generations. The present is the future's past and we try to capture what we're feeling in the moment.

I wish for this book to be used and enjoyed. The experience of making food, of making bread, is a humbling one. Make this bread and savour every moment, enjoy it with those around you. Bring our food to life. Keep our stories alive. And one day we will be all together around a table and can celebrate our cultures.

There is bread and salt between us.

Breads & Topped Breads

One common denominator in all world cuisines is bread. In Lebanon, not a day goes by without bread featuring in at least one meal, and we have different breads for different uses and occasions. Mostly they serve the usual purpose as a vessel for scooping up food or for sopping up leftovers, but they are also used as wraps for fillings or can be topped as open pies.

Making bread can be an event in itself. Historically, the bread makers of families (the women) would gather in the morning around a communal oven to help one another. In Arabic, there is an expression used to describe gossips – *neswen el-forn* ("women of the oven") – and it springs from this tradition of gathering to bake together and share the stories of the day.

The most commonly known form of bread from our region is the pita, a round flatbread that splits into two, forming a pocket inside. Home-style pita is usually thicker, similar to Greek pita, while bakeries can make it as thin as a crêpe. We cut this bread into bite-sized pieces and use them to scoop food from the plate, toast or fry the bread to use in *fattoush* or *fatteh*, or fill it with ingredients to make a wrap. It is worth noting that no one here has *ever* cut a thick pita bread in half and opened it to fill with falafel in such a way that it is impossible to get a bit of the filling in each bite. This is a misappropriation of the bread's function. When ingredients are laid across the diameter of the bread, then wrapped, you are guaranteed to have a fulfilling bite each time.

Tannour and *taboon* flatbreads are less common in towns and cities but are available in some villages. Both require cooking in a large specialist oven. A few traditional bakeries remain, such as Abou Khanjar in Qobayat, a village in North Lebanon not too far from the Syrian border.

A *tannour* oven, which is more commonly found in Lebanon, is a large, deep well dug in the earth in which wood is burned at the bottom to heat up the walls. Bread dough is slapped onto the dampened sides and remains stuck there until it is fully baked, and is then peeled off. The *taboon* oven follows a similar concept but is more common in Palestine. Made of clay and straw moulded into an igloo shape with a top opening, a metal sheet divides the oven in two: the bottom part is where the fuel is burned, pebbles cover the metal sheet on which the dough is baked, and the top of the dome has a lid to trap the heat. Some *taboon* ovens have a side opening in which a tray can be inserted more easily. It is a primitive oven, but some do still exist.

Saj is another old-style bread that survives due to the fact that it is easier to make than *tannour* or *taboon* flatbreads. It is a paper-thin bread made with a soft dough that uses whole wheat and indigenous salamouni wheat flour, which makes it ideal for making *manouche*. It is skillfully tossed between expert hands to reach the thickness needed, before being slapped onto a dome-shaped stove on which the dough takes mere seconds to cook.

Baking is a skill everyone should learn, if not for the basic need to survive, then for the pleasure of it. I have been valuing gatherings around making bread and food even more these days and we have been working as a family to maintain the traditions. We like to make the house a bustling spot on Epiphany Eve for family and friends to come together to cook and share *Zalabye* (page 45), and during the holy week of Easter we make *Ka'ak Asfar* (page 31) and *Maamoul* (pages 132–4). I hope that we will be able to keep these traditions alive for as long as possible, and to keep sharing them with others.

When the economic crisis hit Lebanon in 2019–2020, lots of families stocked up on flour and made their own bread. If we had bread, we felt safe. The making of bread is a little piece of comfort and normality in the midst of chaos and having this basic skill can be a life-saver in times of crisis.

On taboon

This soft, pillowy, dimpled flatbread is a classic Palestinian staple. *Taboon* is one of the most traditional ways of making bread in our region – a centuries-old method of cooking. The *taboon*, or *tabun*, is a rustic portable oven made from straw and hay kneaded with clay, shaped into a dome, then placed over a flat surface, usually a layer of smooth stones. A fire would be lit in the bottom and the dome would trap the heat within until the whole contraption was hot enough for baking. Typically, a wood fire would be lit the night before, then the oven would be sealed and left until charcoal had formed. Once the ashes were cleared from the oven the next day, bread could be baked in the residual heat, either on the hot stones beneath or on a surface placed in the middle of the oven to receive the dough. The flatbread would take the shape of the surface it had been cooked on and would be flavourful and aromatic from the smoky interior of the clay oven.

At the time that I am writing this book, the Palestinian territory of Gaza is under blockade. I have seen footage of the people trapped there resorting to building these types of oven to make their bread as there is a shortage of fuel. They make these ovens from resources they find in the land around them and use any type of material that will burn to fuel the fire – felled trees, used paper cups, wood retrieved from collapsed buildings, even the leaflets dropped before the start of another raid.

People look for anyone making bread in makeshift ways after bakeries have been bombed. We can see the relief and joy on the faces of those who have managed to find fresh bread or a *manouche* on a rainy day. Their plight is dreadful, but their resourcefulness shows how the old techniques remain strongly rooted in our culture.

Taboon bread is not typically made at home anymore, not since the arrival of modern ovens. Today you are more likely to buy it. But I include the following recipe as testament to the traditional Palestinian way of baking. If you can find any, a few smooth river pebbles that have been thoroughly dried and placed on a heavy-duty oven tray will approximate the conditions that can be found in these clay ovens (failing that, use a pizza stone).

Recipe overleaf

Taboon

Palestinian flatbreads

This traditional Palestinian flatbread is soft, pillowy and versatile. It is hard to replicate the unique smoky flavour that it takes on when baked in a traditional taboon oven (see previous page), but you can still make a tasty, soft flatbread in a conventional oven that is ideal as a wrap, or as a base for a Palestinian msakhan (a dish of sumac chicken and onions served on a taboon bread, page 88).

MAKES 6 FLATBREADS

200 g (1⅔ cups) strong (bread) flour

150 g (1 cup) wholewheat (wholemeal) flour, plus extra for dusting (or use cornmeal for dusting)

2 tablespoons fine burghul (optional)

½ teaspoon dried active yeast

1 teaspoon salt

250 ml (1 cup) water

60 ml (¼ cup) olive oil

YOU WILL NEED

clean, dry river pebbles (each about the size of a ping-pong ball, see note)

a sturdy oven tray

OR

a pizza stone

NOTE

River pebbles can be purchased at homewares stores, make sure to purchase stones that do not have any kind of coating on them. Wash and dry them thoroughly before heating. Stones collected from nature should be used with caution as they may contain a small amount of moisture, which can cause them to crack or pop suddenly when heated.

Mix all the dry ingredients in a large bowl. Add the water and half of the olive oil, and mix until you get a shaggy dough.

Knead the dough on the work surface for 5 minutes (or in a stand mixer fitted with a dough hook). Use as little additional flour as possible when kneading.

Drizzle the remaining olive oil into the bowl and return the dough to the bowl. Cover and rest for 1 hour. You can also leave it overnight (8–10 hours) to slow ferment if the temperature is kept low, or place it in the refrigerator.

Divide the dough into 6 equal pieces and shape each one into a ball. Return to the bowl, cover and rest for 10 minutes.

Meanwhile, preheat the oven to 230°C (450°F/gas 8). Arrange the clean and dry pebbles in a sturdy oven tray (or use a pizza stone) and place it at the bottom of the oven to preheat.

On a flour- or cornmeal-dusted work surface, use a rolling pin to roll each ball out into a disc, 5 mm (¼ in) thick. You can even flip it between your hands like pizza dough in a pizzeria. Throw it onto the hot pebbles or pizza stone and bake for 2–3 minutes. If the top hasn't taken on any colour in this time, flip it and bake for a further 1–2 minutes.

Remove from the oven and wrap in a clean dish towel, then repeat to cook the rest of the dough. Allow the flatbreads to cool slightly, if not eating immediately, and store in a plastic bag to preserve their moisture.

Saj
Wafer-thin flatbreads

This crêpe-like bread is made with an unleavened dough that's pressed on a well-floured surface and then flapped swiftly between the palms of both hands until it is the size of the convex metal griddle on which the dough is cooked. Or sometimes it might be laid on a round pillow that allows the baker to stretch the dough even further before transporting the pillow and slapping it to stick the dough over the griddle. The dough is paper-thin, so barely a few seconds will pass before it is done – enough time for a skilled baker to spread and flap another dough ball to be ready for baking.

The mother of a friend of mine told me that the best flour for saj is an indigenous variety called salamouni, *which is a hard grain like durum wheat. Making this bread is a fading skill and only acquired by people from rural villages, refugees and skilled workers. Despite that, I think the demand is still good enough for more people to learn it and for bakers to continue to make it.*

MAKES 10–12 PIECES

200 g (1⅔ cups) strong (bread) flour

300 g (2 cups) wholewheat (wholemeal) flour

1 teaspoon instant dried yeast

10 g (generous 1½ teaspoons) salt

300–350 ml (scant 1¼–generous 1⅓ cups) water

2 tablespoons olive oil, for greasing

100 g (⅔ cup) plain (all-purpose) flour, for dusting

YOU WILL NEED

a *saj* griddle (or upturned wok or heavy frying pan)

a *saj* cushion (or cover a regular cushion with a clean pillowcase)

In a bowl or a stand mixer, mix the flours, yeast and salt, then add 300 ml (scant 1¼ cups) of the water and mix until incorporated, adding more water if needed. Wholewheat flour can absorb more water, but the dough might not need a lot more water, so measure with your eyes and hands until you reach a dough that's a little loose but can hold its shape. Knead the dough for 6–8 minutes (8–10 if kneading by hand) until the dough is elastic. Don't be discouraged if the dough is still a bit loose. Cover it and rest for 20 minutes.

Stretch out one side of the dough and fold it over the rest of the dough. Give the bowl a quarter turn and repeat. Repeat the stretching, folding and turning with all four sides of the dough. If the dough is still very loose at this stage you can repeat this step on the spot, otherwise cover and rest for another 20 minutes before repeating again. Once a firm dough is achieved, grease a clean bowl with the oil, add the dough, then cover and leave to rise for 1 hour.

When ready to bake, heat your baking apparatus. Traditionally a *saj* (a domed griddle) is used, but if one is not available use an upside-down wok (cover the handles with foil to protect them if they're made of wood) or use a large frying pan, which will yield a different bread, but close enough.

Divide the dough into 10–12 pieces and roll each into a ball. Place the dough balls back into the greased bowl while flattening out each piece of dough.

Generously flour the work surface with the plain flour, sometimes a ½ cup is placed on the work surface to use for multiple dough balls. Coat a dough ball in the flour and press it with your palm to flatten. Thin out the outer edges of the disc by pressing and turning the disc until the sides are thinner than

the centre. Next, flap the dough between your palms as if you're tossing it from one palm to the other – rather like tossing pizza dough. This will allow the dough to stretch to the desired size and thinness – it should be really thin, paper thin, and should fit onto your baking apparatus. If a *saj* cushion is not available, prepare one by covering a cushion with a clean pillowcase on which to transfer your dough. If possible, stretch the dough out even further, then use the cushion to slap the dough onto the hot baking apparatus. Alternatively, transfer it by hand to the heated pan. Allow the dough to cook for 30 seconds, or until it no longer looks like raw dough. If it's not very thin, it might be necessary to flip it, cooking it for another 30 seconds or until it is cooked through.

Remove the cooked bread from the heat and spray with water, then cover with a clean dish towel. If the bread is properly thin, moisture must be added back to make the bread pliable, otherwise it will be stiff and easily broken, like a wafer.

Repeat with the remaining dough balls.

Store the bread in a sealed bag. It is best consumed within 2–3 days and can be refrigerated or frozen.

Meshtah Ramadan

Aniseed bread for Ramadan

During Ramadan, Muslims fast for as long as the sun is in the sky, from the moment the sun peeks over the horizon until the moment it hides behind it on the other side (indeed, some wait until all the light has disappeared to break their fast). To sustain them during this long period, especially when Ramadan takes place between the March and September equinox when the daytime is long, fasting individuals are woken up before the fajr (daybreak) prayer by a musaharaty (a person who wakes the neighbourhood up by beating a drum) to have a small meal and beverage before starting the fast. Meshtah Ramadan is a common bread to have at this meal, known as the suhur, with labneh and vegetables, a cup of tea and plenty of water. Meshtah can be easily found in Lebanese bakeries in areas with a large number of Muslim residents, and is only made during Ramadan.

MAKES 2 x 25 CM (10 IN) LOAVES

500 g (3⅓ cups) strong (bread) flour (or a mixture of plain/all-purpose and strong/bread flour), plus extra for dusting

90 g (½ cup) fine burghul soaked in 125 ml (½ cup) water (optional)

1 tablespoon white granulated sugar

1½ teaspoons salt

1 teaspoon instant dried yeast

1 teaspoon ground mahlab

1 teaspoon whole aniseeds (or ½ teaspoon ground aniseed)

275 ml (1 cup plus 2 generous tablespoons) water, milk or milk whey

50 ml (scant ¼ cup) olive oil, plus extra for brushing

1 tablespoon sesame seeds

1 tablespoon nigella seeds

In a large bowl, mix all the ingredients, except the sesame and nigella seeds. Mix until a dough comes together, then turn out onto a floured work surface and knead for 3–5 minutes. (Alternatively, this can be done in a stand mixer fitted with a dough hook.) Place back in the bowl, cover with a damp dish towel and set aside to prove for at least 1–2 hours.

Preheat the oven to 200°C (400°F/gas 6). Grease 2 baking sheets with olive oil.

Take the dough out of the bowl and divide in half. Roughly roll each piece into a ball. Place on the prepared baking sheets and stretch out to 3 cm (1 in) thick ovals. Cover with a damp dish towel and leave to rest for 15–20 minutes.

Just before baking, brush each loaf with olive oil, sprinkle with the sesame and nigella seeds, and dimple the surface of each loaf with your fingers.

Bake for 15 minutes until golden brown.

This is best eaten when freshly baked. Alternatively, cool and store the bread in a sealed container or bag for 2–3 days, or freeze.

Ka'ak Asfar

Palestinian yellow Easter bread

A Palestinian Christian tradition, we make this bread on the Saturday between Good Friday and Easter Sunday. Some claim it is made this way to resemble the large stone covering Christ's tomb. In the refugee camp where I was raised, everyone around us would be making this bread on that day. The narrow hillside streets were filled with people who had prepared their dough for proving and either started heating their ovens at home or booked an appointment at the nearby bakery to bake this blessing of the Easter holiday. Wherever you walked in the camp on that day you would be welcomed by the smell of freshly baked bread coated in olive oil and the aromas of the spices used in the dough: nutty mahlab and distinct, warming turmeric.

My family's tradition was to bake the bread on Saturday and, after the Easter dawn mass at the local church, have it for breakfast at my grandma's house. We would do this right up until she passed away. We still maintain an Easter meal of Ka'ak Asfar and Easter eggs with labneh and olives each year with my parents, sisters and invited guests.

MAKES 10–12 PIECES

1 kg (6⅔ cups) plain (all-purpose) flour
1 tablespoon instant dried yeast
1 tablespoon ground mahlab
2 tablespoons ground aniseed
1 tablespoon ground turmeric
⅛ teaspoon ground nutmeg
⅛ teaspoon ground cloves
2 tablespoons sesame seeds
1 tablespoon nigella seeds
20 g (generous 1 tablespoon) salt
400–600 ml (1⅔–2⅓ cups) water
  (or as needed)
60 ml (¼ cup) vegetable oil
olive oil, for coating

Mix all the dry ingredients in a large bowl. Add 400 ml (1⅔ cups) of the water along with the vegetable oil and knead until you reach a firm dough, adding more water as needed to create a smooth, soft dough. Coat the dough with a good layer of olive oil, cover with cling film (plastic wrap) and leave to rise until doubled in size (around 45 minutes–1 hour, this time will depend on the ambient temperature in your kitchen).

Preheat the oven to 200°C (400°F/gas 6).

Take a handful of dough and form it into a small ball, coat with more olive oil and set aside. Repeat with the whole batch until you have 10–12 balls. Roll the balls into around 18 cm (7 in) discs or directly press them over a *ka'ak* mould for this kind of bread (if you don't have a mould you can use the bottom of a clean colander to give the bread a pattern and keep it flat).

Place the discs of dough on a baking sheet and bake in the oven until the tops and bottoms are lightly browned. Remove and brush generously with olive oil.

Serve warm with labneh and boiled eggs.

Ka'ak asfar can be stored in the freezer for 6 months. Defrost thoroughly and heat well before serving.

Qorban

Orthodox holy bread

This ancient leavened bread recipe dates back to the Byzantine period. Growing up Christian in Lebanon, it was mandatory to participate in the Sunday mass at least. Most Palestinians are Melkite Greek Catholics, and instead of a thin plain wafer for communion bread (as you might find elsewhere) here the communion is taken with a plain soft loaf that is cut into pieces and dipped in sweet wine diluted with water. Certain churches offer a similar bread, cut into fist-sized chunks from a large loaf and distributed at the end of mass in baskets as a blessing. It is often marked with a special stamp or mould, but homemade versions can be simpler, with a pattern of holes made in the surface of the bread instead.

I used to buy this bread from a bakery in a village up in the mountains called Al Khenchara. As well as making the communion bread, which is nothing but flour, yeast and water, they also made another bread which is soft and lightly fragrant with orange blossom water and mastic. I like to eat it on its own, but sometimes I slice it in half and fill it with peanut butter and jam (I hope no one gets mad at me for that!).

Pound the sugar and mastic together in a pestle and mortar until powdered. Sift together with the mahlab.

In a large bowl, combine all the ingredients and knead until a dough comes together. Cover and set aside to rest and rise for about 30 minutes, or until doubled in size (this time will depend on the ambient temperature in your kitchen).

Preheat the oven to 200°C (400°F/gas 6).

Scrape the dough from the sides of the bowl, turn out onto a floured surface and divide in half. Roll each portion into a ball, dust with flour and place on a tray large enough to fit both dough balls (remembering the dough will rise more). Dust the tops with more flour, cover with a clean dish towel and leave to rise for 15 minutes.

Stick your finger or the end of a wooden spoon into some flour and poke 5 holes into the dough, forming the shape that the number 5 does on dice. Alternatively, you can score or press a pattern in the surface with the tip of a sharp knife.

Bake in the oven for 15–20 minutes until golden brown.

Remove from the tray and leave to cool on a wire rack or a dish towel. Store in a plastic bag or airtight container for up to 4 days, or freeze for up to 1 month.

MAKES 2 LOAVES

1 tablespoon white granulated sugar

4 pieces of mastic (total equivalent to size of 2 lentils)

1 tablespoon ground mahlab

500 g (3⅓ cups) strong (bread) or plain (all-purpose) flour, plus extra for dusting

1 teaspoon instant dried yeast

1 teaspoon salt

3 tablespoons orange blossom water

300 ml (scant 1¼ cups) water

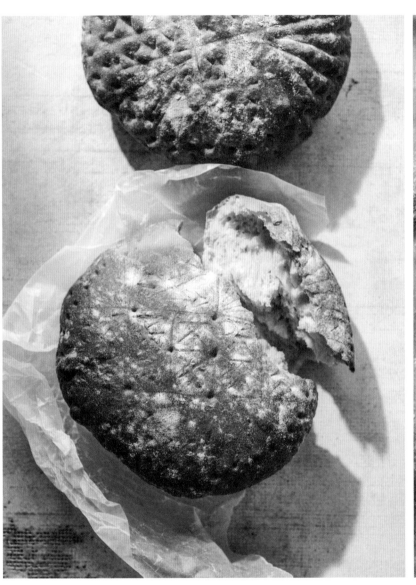

Maronite Qorban

Maronite holy bread buns

In Maronite churches, the largest Christian sect in Lebanon, thin wafers are used for communion. But after funerals in almost all churches, people offer their condolences by shaking the hands of the family of the deceased and at the end of the line there is a person handing out tea-plate-sized buns in sealed, clear plastic packs. These buns differ from the ones used in Greek liturgies in that they are sweeter and use more aromatics; sometimes they contain milk and have a glazed, golden top.

There used to be two bakeries in the refugee camp where I grew up that made these buns for funerals. We always preferred the ones from Nassim, the baker down the street. We would know when he was baking qorban as the scent of orange blossom, mastic and freshly baked and glazed bread would fill the air. Although qorban are synonymous with someone's passing, getting to enjoy them at the end of the service was something small to look forward to.

Pound the sugar and mastic together in a pestle and mortar until powdered.

In a large bowl, combine all the ingredients, except the oil and flower waters for brushing. Knead until a dough comes together. Cover and set aside to rest and rise for about 30 minutes, or until doubled in size (this time will depend on the ambient temperature in your kitchen).

Preheat the oven to 200°C (400°F/gas 6).

Scrape the dough from the sides of the bowl, turn out onto a floured surface and divide into 6 portions. Roll each portion into a ball, dust with flour and place on baking trays, leaving enough space for the dough to expand. Dust the tops with more flour, cover with a clean dish towel and leave to rise for 15 minutes.

Poke 5 holes in the middle of each bun with a wooden skewer, forming the shape that the number 5 does on dice.

Bake in the oven for 15–20 minutes until golden brown.

Mix the remaining orange blossom water with the rose water. As soon as the buns are removed from the oven, brush them with the flower waters. Remove from the tray and leave to cool on a wire rack or a dish towel. Store in a plastic bag or airtight container for up to 4 days, or freeze for up to 1 month.

MAKES 6 BUNS

55 g (¼ cup) white granulated sugar

4 pieces of mastic (total equivalent to size of 2 lentils)

500 g (3⅓ cups) plain (all-purpose) flour, plus extra for dusting

1 teaspoon instant dried yeast

1 teaspoon salt

250 ml (1 cup) water (or use an aniseed infusion with 1 tablespoon aniseeds)

2 tablespoons milk powder (or 50 ml/ 3 tablespoons full-fat milk)

60 ml (¼ cup) orange blossom water, plus 1 tablespoon for brushing

2 tablespoons vegetable or olive oil

1 tablespoon rose water, for brushing

Ka'ak Al-Qods

Jerusalem sesame bagels

I have never been to Al-Qods (the Arabic name for Jerusalem) and I don't think in my lifetime I'll be allowed to go there, but I hope to. They say that a lot of bakeries have made this bread outside of Al-Qods but I think it would be extra special to eat this in Al-Qods. Whether that is due to pure nostalgia and emotion – or whether there is an actual biological reason (possibly the yeast or natural bacteria in the air or the elevation or the water) – I do not know. But we can at least try to recreate the pleasure of having ka'ak Al-Qods at home. This ka'ak is soft yet chewy with a hint of sweetness from the honey or molasses coating and a crunchy sesame crust. I also add a little bit of mahlab because I like the flavour it brings to baked goods.

MAKES 8

1 teaspoon ground mahlab

350 g (2⅓ cups) plain (all-purpose) flour

150 g (1 cup) strong (bread) flour

1¼ teaspoons salt

2 tablespoons white granulated sugar

1½ teaspoons instant dried yeast

350 ml (generous 1⅓ cups) water or milk

2 tablespoons olive oil, plus extra as needed

1 tablespoon grape molasses (or another thin molasses or honey)

2 tablespoons warm water

120 g (generous ¾ cup) sesame seeds

TO SERVE

white cheese

labneh

a tray of olives and pickles

black tea

Sift the mahlab to remove any lumps. Add to the bowl of a stand mixer fitted with a dough hook and mix with the flours, salt, sugar and yeast. Add the water or milk and mix for 5–7 minutes until the dough is elastic. Add a tablespoon of the olive oil, then scoop the dough out of the bowl and knead for 1 minute on the work surface, using extra oil to prevent sticking, if needed. Return to the bowl with another tablespoon of oil. Cover and leave to rest for 1 hour, or until doubled in size.

Remove the dough from the bowl and divide it into 8 pieces (or more if you want smaller *ka'ak*), then shape into balls. Cover again and leave to rest for 10 minutes.

Meanwhile, preheat the oven to 200°C (400°F/gas 6).

Mix the grape molasses with the warm water until completely dissolved. Add the sesame seeds and mix well, making sure the mixture is not runny.

Take each dough ball and poke a hole in its centre, then stretch it to the desired size and thickness (elongated oval rings are traditional, but rounds are good too). Coat all over with the sesame mixture and place on a baking sheet. Cover and rest for 10–15 minutes until increased in size.

Bake for 15–20 minutes until golden brown.

Cool and serve, or break apart while still warm and serve with white cheese, labneh, a tray of olives and pickles, and some black tea.

Akras Bil Zaytoun

Olive and chilli bread rolls

A traditional bread recipe from Palestine is qras bi za'atar, which are like flatbreads (similar to naan), but made with the local oregano that the za'atar mix is made from. Taking that idea as a starting point, I made this recipe by puréeing green olives and chillies to a paste to use as a filling, adding dried oregano to the dough (fresh za'atar would work well too), and rolling the dough like you would a cinnamon roll before baking. I could have eaten the whole batch with nothing on it, but I had to save some to scoop up some labneh.

In a large mixing bowl, combine the flour, yeast, sugar, salt and oregano. Add the liquid and 1 tablespoon of the olive oil and knead until you get a shaggy dough. Transfer to the work surface and knead for 10 minutes until the dough is firm.

Use another 1 tablespoon of the olive oil to oil the bowl, put the dough back in the bowl and turn to coat in the oil, then cover and leave to rise for 1 hour, or until doubled in size.

Punch the dough down and divide into 6 equal pieces. Roll each piece into a ball, place back in the oiled bowl, cover and leave to prove for 10 minutes.

Preheat the oven to 200°C (400°F/gas 6).

Pulse the garlic and chillies with the remaining 1 tablespoon of the olive oil in a food processor until finely chopped. Add the olives and blitz until roughly chopped. (If you wish, you can add herbs or some puréed sun-dried tomatoes to the mix at this point.) Divide the filling into 6 equal parts.

Oil the work surface, then roll each dough ball out as thinly as possible to a wide rectangular shape with the long edges facing you. Spread one-sixth of the filling over each rectangle, leaving the long edge furthest away from you clear of filling. Roll up the dough from the edge closest to you until you get a long rope and pinch the edges closed. Roll in each end towards the middle, then tuck one of the coils under the other to create a snail shape.

Generously brush a baking tray with olive oil, arrange the rolls in the tray and brush with more olive oil. Bake for 20–23 minutes, or until puffed and golden and the rolls feel light rather than dense.

Remove from the oven and brush with more olive oil (or generously spray with water from a spray bottle). Serve warm, or cover once cooled and store in an airtight container for up to 3 days.

MAKES 6

350 g (2⅓ cups) strong (bread) flour

1 teaspoon instant dried yeast

1 teaspoon white granulated sugar

½ teaspoon salt

2 teaspoons dried oregano

200 ml (generous ¾ cup) water
(or milk or yoghurt whey from making labneh)

3 tablespoons olive oil, plus extra for brushing

1 garlic clove, peeled

25 g (1 oz) whole red chillies
(deseeded, if wished)

175 g (scant 1½ cups) pitted green olives
(or black, if you prefer)

Ma'arouk

Sweet stuffed brioche

MAKES 4 (15 CM) OR 6 (10 CM) BUNS

FOR THE DOUGH

400 g (2⅔ cups) plain (all-purpose)
   flour, plus extra for dusting

2 teaspoons instant dried yeast

80 g (scant ⅓ cup) white
   granulated sugar

2 teaspoons ground mahlab

1 teaspoon salt

1 egg

50 g (1¾ oz) soft butter (or olive oil)

250 ml (1 cup) milk (or water)

FOR THE DATE FILLING

400 g (14 oz) date paste (or mashed
   pitted dates)

1 teaspoon ground cinnamon

½ teaspoon ground nutmeg

3 tablespoons olive oil (or butter)

FOR THE COCONUT FILLING

125 g (2 cups) unsweetened
   shredded coconut

125 g (generous ½ cup) white
   granulated sugar

100 g (generous ¾ cup) raisins

60–80 ml (¼–⅓ cup) water (or brandy)

FOR THE CHOCOLATE-ALMOND FILLING

150 g (5 oz) dark chocolate (60%
   cocoa solids; or use a less bitter type
   and adjust the sugar, or use milk
   chocolate and skip the sugar),
   finely chopped

80 g (½ cup) almonds, coarsely chopped

60 g (¼ cup) white granulated sugar

FOR THE TOPPING

1 egg

1 tablespoon olive oil (or milk)

50 g (⅓ cup) sesame seeds

NOTE

If making all three fillings, you will need
to triple the amount of dough.

I grew up waiting to hear the piercing horn of the Ka'ak-seller's bicycle honking as he went down the street on Saturday mornings. I'd jump out of bed, grab some money and yell out for the man on the bicycle to stop. Of course, he would have ka'ak asrouniye, sesame-covered thin bread purses (the recipe is in my first book), but I preferred the softer and fluffier brioche-style loaves, especially for their sweet fillings, to have with a cup of coffee in the morning. If he had stopped for me, I would first check if he still had one of the coconut-filled loaves; if not, I would get a date-filled one. The date stuffing recipe I give here is pretty authentic, but I played around a little with the coconut version, and completely made up the chocolate-almond filling to my taste. I hope you like them too.

Combine all the dough ingredients in a bowl or a stand mixer and mix by hand or with the dough hook until you have a slightly sticky dough. Cover and set aside to prove for around 1 hour (this time will depend on the ambient temperature of your kitchen).

Dust your work surface with a handful of flour, then scrape the dough onto it. Gently fold it into the flour to coat and cut the dough into 4 or 6 equal pieces. Roll each piece into a ball, dust with flour and cover with cling film (plastic wrap) or a damp dish towel and leave to rest for 10 minutes.

Preheat the oven to 200°C (400°F/gas 6).

Mix the filling ingredients of your choice and set aside.

Take a dough ball and press it out to a disc. Lift and stretch the dough, if needed. Divide the filling according to how many pieces of dough you have. Scoop one portion into the middle of the disc and fold in the edges of the dough to cover the filling. Flip and press gently to seal the bottom and spread the filling. Transfer to a baking sheet lined with baking paper. Fill and shape the rest of the dough pieces in the same way. Cover with a damp dish towel and leave to rest and prove for a further 10–15 minutes.

Mix the egg and olive oil or milk for the topping and brush the tops of the proved dough with the mixture. Sprinkle with plenty of sesame seeds.

Bake for 10 minutes, or until golden. Remove from the oven and spray the surface of the dough with water (this will help the buns soften once cooled). Leave to cool.

Store in a sealed container for up to 3 days, or freeze and reheat in the oven when needed.

Zalabye

Spiced fried dough for Epiphany

These fried dough rings are a speciality that Palestinians prepare on the night of Epiphany (5 January), the night where we commemorate the baptism of Christ in the River Jordan. They are lightly seasoned with anise, mahlab, and sesame and nigella seeds. We make the dough and let it rise, but before starting to fry the dough, we wrap small portions of it and place them outside on a tree that's not a fig or mulberry. The dough portions will sit there throughout the night with a candle or a light on it in the belief that Christ passes around midnight, with trees bowing to Him, to bless the dough that people will use for the coming year. To me that sounds like a basic sourdough starter – a blessed one though.

Many traditions and blessings are linked to the feast of Epiphany at the beginning of the year. My mom makes zalabye every year and we all gather to share the blessing of the holiday. The streets fill with the aromas everywhere you go and we've been gathering an audience every year to come and enjoy them fresh out of the fryer. We serve zalabye with plates of labneh drizzled in olive oil and with bitter green olives. Lebanese people make zlebye (same thing; slightly different pronunciation) with fewer spices or aromatics and dust them with powdered sugar or a drizzle of molasses. I prefer the savoury style.

SERVES 4

500 g (3⅓ cups) plain (all-purpose) flour
1½ teaspoons ground mahlab
1 tablespoon ground aniseed
1 tablespoon sesame
1½ teaspoons nigella seeds
1 teaspoon white granulated sugar
½ teaspoon salt
1 teaspoon instant dried yeast
1–1½ cups water
neutral oil, for deep-frying
labneh or molasses, to serve

In a large bowl, mix all the dry ingredients, then gradually add the water and knead until the mixture comes together into a soft dough. Cover with cling film (plastic wrap) and leave to rise for 1–2 hours.

Before starting to work with the dough, fill a large saucepan with a 5 cm (2 in) depth of oil for deep-frying and heat until hot.

With wet hands, pinch a piece of the dough and roll it into a ball. Set aside on a damp surface to prevent sticking.

Take another, larger pinch and roll it into a ball, then stretch it, hollowing the centre to form a ring just larger than the first prepared ball. Place it around the ball and continue to form larger rings until you reach the size you want.

Start the frying by carefully dropping the small ball into the hot oil, then carefully add the rings around it, one by one. Have someone next to you with a skewer or a pair of tongs to keep the rings in place. Fry until golden in colour, then carefully flip, holding the whole disc with a large pair of tongs, and fry until golden all over.

Remove and drain on kitchen paper. Serve with either labneh or molasses.

Manouchet Za'atar

Za'atar-topped breads

This is the most basic and most readily available of all manouche. Before school started or during recess, this was our breakfast or lunch (with a pyramid carton of Bonjus juice). It was economical – the cheese manouche was pricier and we'd have to save for it. Later, when I got a job and would have to wake up early to get there on time, I used to grab a manouche from the nearby bakery when I didn't have time for breakfast. I believe the za'atar manouche in its simplest form is the best: soft dough with aromatic olive oil and a za'atar mix with local oregano, sumac, lightly toasted sesame seeds and salt. I would add sliced cucumber and tomatoes, lots of mint and black olives. Thinly sliced onions are a controversial addition, but can be really delicious. Serve as part of a breakfast spread with fresh vegetables and tea.

In a large bowl, combine the flour with the salt, sugar and yeast. Make a well in the middle, add the warm water and olive oil and mix with a wooden spoon or your hands. Knead until the dough comes together away from the sides of the bowl. Coat the ball of dough with a little oil, cover the bowl with a dish towel and leave to prove in a warm place for 1 hour or until doubled in size.

Meanwhile, preheat the oven to 200°C (400°F/gas 6) and place a baking sheet in the oven to heat up.

Punch down the risen dough and turn out onto a lightly floured work surface. Divide into 6 pieces and shape each piece into a ball by pinching the sides down and rolling in the palm of one hand against the work surface. Cover again and let rest for 10 minutes. Lightly flour the surface and rolling pin, then roll the dough balls into circles 8–10 mm (½ in) thick. Cover and leave to rest for a further 10 minutes.

Mix together the za'atar and olive oil for the topping.

Poke the dough rounds with a fork or dimple with your fingers to prevent them from puffing up, then spread each with a tablespoon of the za'atar mixture. Bake on the hot baking sheet for about 8 minutes until the dough is lightly browned and cooked through. Serve warm.

Pictured with Cheese & pepper paste manouche (page 49)

MAKES 6

FOR THE DOUGH

350 g (2⅓ cups) strong (bread) flour, plus extra for dusting

1 teaspoon fine salt

1 teaspoon caster (superfine) sugar (or honey)

2 teaspoons instant dried yeast

200 ml (generous ¾ cup) warm water

60 ml (¼ cup) olive oil, plus extra for coating

FOR THE TOPPING

30 g (around 6 tablespoons) za'atar

90 ml (6 tablespoons) olive oil

Manouchet Jebne

Cheese *manouche*

In a foodie conversation in Lebanon, if you have survived the dividing question of whether you're a tabbouleh or fattoush person, you may then be asked if you're a za'atar or jebne (cheese) manouche person. You could choose to take a diplomatic route and say you like a "cocktail", with half the manouche spread with the za'atar and oil mix and the other half with cheese. I don't mind – I won't have strong feelings if you choose that. I save my scorn for more serious issues, like messing with tabbouleh, for example. Or butchering our recipes and presenting them as authentic! But back to the manouche...

This manouche can change drastically depending on the cheese you use. The best type to use is Akkawi cheese, which – as the name suggests – comes from Akka, Palestine. The regular Akkawi cheese is a firm white cheese, while the Czech-style is even firmer with a salty brine. The latter needs to be soaked in water and rinsed to soften the saltiness. You will find the same cheese used in sweets, such as Knefe (page 121). If you can't find it, you can replace it with a mix of mozzarella and a little feta for saltiness.

Follow the recipe for making the *manouche* dough on page 46, dividing and rolling the dough into 4 rounds, about 5 mm (¼ in) thick, and resting as directed.

Preheat the oven to 200°C (400°F/gas 6) and place a baking sheet in the oven to heat up.

If using Czech Akkawi cheese, shred it and rinse it with cold water a couple of times until it is less salty. If using mozzarella or other cheeses, shred them and set aside.

Poke shallow holes into the dough rounds with a fork or dimple with your fingers to prevent them from puffing up. Divide the shredded cheese among the dough rounds and transfer to the baking sheet. Bake for 6–8 minutes, or until the cheese has melted and starts to brown a little.

Remove from the oven and cool a little before serving. These are best served hot, but there is also pleasure in eating them cold as well. Serve with vegetables, herbs, olives and pickles with a side of black tea or aniseed infusion. Store leftovers in the refrigerator or freezer and reheat when needed. These can be frozen for up to a month.

MAKES 4

1 × quantity *manouche* dough
(page 46)
500 g (1 lb 2 oz) Czech Akkawi cheese
(or mozzarella combined with a salty
cheese like feta)

TO SERVE
vegetables
herbs
a tray of olives and pickles
black tea or aniseed infusion

Cheese & Pepper Paste Manouche

Muhammara *is a mezze item that originates in Syrian and Aleppo-Armenian cuisine, which made its way into Lebanese mezze. It is made from roasted bell peppers with walnuts, pomegranate molasses and occasionally breadcrumbs. It makes a great topping for* manouche. *A quick cheat to make your own would be to use a ready-made pepper paste, adjusting the heat level to your liking, then mixing it with the same ingredients. An even better cheat, as I've done here, is to simply use pure pepper paste as a base, spread it over the* manouche *dough, top it with cheese and bake. You can also find this combination as a filling for ka'ak (the sesame-covered, purse-shaped breads I talked about in my first book,* Bayrut), *at specialised* ka'ak *shops as a quick delicious pick-me-up breakfast or snack.*

Follow the recipe for making the *manouche* dough on page 46, dividing and rolling the dough into 4 rounds, about 5 mm (¼ in) thick, and resting as directed.

Preheat the oven to 200°C (400°F/gas 6) and place a baking sheet in the oven to heat up.

If using Czech Akkawi cheese, shred it and rinse it with cold water a couple of times until it is less salty. If using mozzarella or other cheeses, shred them and set aside.

Poke shallow holes into the dough rounds with a fork or dimple with your fingers to prevent them from puffing up. Spread the pepper paste mix over each round, covering almost all the dough surface but leaving a 5 mm (¼ in) border around the circumference, like spreading pizza sauce. Divide the shredded cheese among the rounds and transfer to the baking sheet. Bake for 6–8 minutes, or until the cheese has melted and starts to brown a little.

Remove from the oven and cool a little before serving. These are best served hot, but there is also pleasure in eating them cold as well. Serve with vegetables, herbs, olives and pickles with a side of black tea or aniseed infusion. Store leftovers in the refrigerator or freezer and reheat when needed. These can be frozen for up to a month.

MAKES 4

1 × quantity *manouche* dough
  (page 46)
500 g (1 lb 2 oz) Czech Akkawi cheese
  (or mozzarella combined with a salty
  cheese like feta)
100–150 g (3½–5 oz) red pepper paste
  (sweet or spicy, as you like; or use
  a mix of tomato paste and pepper
  paste; or use *muhammara,* page 67)

TO SERVE
vegetables
herbs
a tray of olives and pickles
black tea or aniseed infusion

Manouchet Bayd bi Awarma

Manouche with eggs, *awarma* and cheese

A trip to Baskinta, a village up the mountains of Lebanon at the foot of the majestic Mount Sannine, is not complete without a visit to Krikor. An old bakery tucked under a grape vine and tall pine trees, it is a destination people frequent for the special manouche *that owner Krikor and his wife Laure make. I chose to recreate one of my favourites: a soft dough topped with a flavourful mix of lamb confit (awarma), eggs and lots of cheese. It's like a cheesy meat omelette/pizza. It is very filling by itself, but can be shared as part of a breakfast or lunch spread with fresh vegetables, pickles, olives and black tea.*

In a bowl, mix together the flour, yeast, salt, sugar and water with a wooden spoon or in a stand mixer fitted with a dough hook until a shaggy dough comes together. Knead on the work surface or in the mixer until a smooth dough forms, around 5 minutes.

Coat the inside of the mixing bowl with the olive oil, turn the ball of dough in it to coat and cover with cling film (plastic wrap). Set aside to prove for 30 minutes–1 hour until doubled in size (this time will depend on the ambient temperature in your kitchen).

Punch down the dough and scrape it out onto a floured work surface. Divide into 4 pieces. Roll each piece into a ball, dust with flour and cover with a clean dish towel. Leave to rest for 15 minutes.

Preheat the oven to the highest temperature (250°C/500°F/gas 10, more if possible). Place a pizza stone or a baking sheet on the middle shelf to heat up.

Generously dust the work surface with cornmeal. Toss a dough ball in the cornmeal to coat, then flatten it with the heel of your palm and stretch from the centre outwards to about 30 cm (12 in) in diameter. You can also lift the dough and let gravity pull it down to stretch it. Place on a board sprinkled with cornmeal. Spread 30 g (1 oz/around 2 tablespoons) of the *awarma* on top of the dough, then cover with a little cheese, around 30 g (1 oz). Crack an egg in the centre and whisk it with a fork, incorporating some of the cheese, until well combined. Cover with more cheese, around 90 g (3 oz).

Once the oven is hot, switch it to the grill (broiler) setting and slide the dough from the board to the hot stone or baking sheet. Cook for 5 minutes, or until the cheese has melted and browned. If the bottom is set but not browned, heat a wide frying pan on the stovetop and cook until slightly browned on the base.

Repeat to cook all your *manouche*. Cut into pieces and serve hot.

MAKES 4

350 g (2⅓ cups) strong (bread) flour, plus extra for dusting

1 teaspoon instant dried yeast

1 teaspoon fine salt

1 teaspoon caster (superfine) sugar

225 ml (7½ fl oz) water (or more if needed)

1 tablespoon olive oil

cornmeal, for dusting

120 g (4 oz) *awarma* (lamb confit – buy in Middle Eastern delis or online; or substitute with sausage meat, *soujok* or other ground spiced meats)

500 g (1 lb 2 oz) mozzarella or Akkawi cheese, grated

4 eggs

Manouchet Shakshouka

Tomato, onion and red pepper paste *manouche*

A little unconventional, but why not? Shakshouka is a dish with mixed roots that is heavily appropriated in numerous cultures. This dish of cooked tomatoes, sometimes with peppers and eggs poached in the sauce, is attributed to Morocco and similar versions are cooked in Algeria, Tunisia, Libya, Turkey, Yemen, and even Italy and Spain, with so many versions in many more countries. A similar version is cooked throughout the regions of Lebanon, Syria, Palestine and Jordan, called qallayet banadoura, *which means "sautéed" or "stewed tomatoes". The dish is simple and doesn't require a lot of ingredients, and can be eaten with bread to make a filling meal. In Syria and Lebanon, a similar dish is called* jazmaz, *where the eggs are scrambled in the tomato sauce. Here, it makes a fun topping for delicious* manouche.

Follow the recipe for making the *manouche* dough on page 46, dividing and rolling the dough into 4 rounds, about 5 mm (¼ in) thick, and resting as directed.

Preheat the oven to 200°C (400°F/gas 6).

Transfer the dough rounds to a baking sheet and slightly pinch the sides of the dough up to create a 2–3 mm (⅛ in) raised edge to hold the filling inside. Poke shallow holes into the dough rounds with a fork or dimple with your fingers to prevent them from puffing up. Spread the pepper paste mix over the base of each round, all the way up to the ridge. Break 2 eggs into the middle of each round and scramble with a fork, then divide the sliced onions among them. (Alternatively, scramble the eggs in a bowl with the onions, then pour into the dough rounds and try to spread it equally).

Bake for around 8 minutes, or until the eggs reach the desired consistency.

Garnish with coriander leaves and sliced spring onions, then cut into 4 or 6 slices and serve hot.

The dough can be half baked with the paste and stored for later (refrigerated or frozen). They can also be baked in a hot frying pan with the filling added in the same way, with a lid placed on top to cook the eggs.

MAKES 4

1 × quantity *manouche* dough (page 46)

150 g (5 oz) red pepper paste (sweet or spicy, as you like) mixed with 50 g (2 oz) tomato paste

8 eggs

100 g (3½ oz) onion, thinly sliced

handful of coriander (cilantro) leaves, chopped, to garnish

2–4 spring onions (scallions), thinly sliced, to garnish

Manouchet Harr

Onion and red pepper *manouche*

I have never been served this recipe by anyone except my mom and I have rarely seen it made and served this way by non-Palestinians. It was one of the things I grew to like, but didn't like when I was younger – I had issues with onions and didn't want to see them on my plate, neither raw nor cooked. But I wouldn't mind them if I couldn't see them! I grew out of it.

This differs slightly from the muhammara or pepper paste manouche (page 49) in that the topping is made from lots of onions and peppers. The whole thing is cooked until the onions soften and the topping becomes thick and spreadable. Plenty of olive oil brings out the flavour.

Follow the recipe for making the *manouche* dough on page 46, dividing and rolling the dough into 6 rounds and resting as directed.

Preheat the oven to 200°C (400°F/gas 6) and place a baking sheet in the oven to heat up.

For the topping, pulse the onions and peppers together with the pepper paste and salt in a food processor until finely chopped.

Heat the olive oil in a small saucepan over a medium heat, add the pepper mixture and cook until the liquid evaporates. Set aside to cool.

Prick the dough rounds all over with a fork or dimple with your fingers to prevent them from puffing up, then spread each with a tablespoon of the topping. Bake on the hot baking sheet for about 8 minutes until the dough is lightly browned and cooked through. Serve warm.

MAKES 6

1 × quantity *manouche* dough
(page 46)
250 g (9 oz) onions, peeled
350 g (12½ oz) red bell peppers,
trimmed and deseeded
2 tablespoons red pepper paste
2 teaspoons salt
60 ml (¼ cup) olive oil

Lahm Baajine

Topped cracker-thin flatbreads

In my first book, Bayrut, I explored the different versions of meats baked on or in dough. Lahm baajine is a ubiquitous and the most basic form of that combination – a very thin dough topped with spiced raw meat and baked just enough for the meat to cook. A common practice is to serve lahm baajine before or after funerals, which leads to a joke about people going to funerals just to get free lahm baajine. Rather like manouche, it is a common quick breakfast or lunch.

My mom used to prepare the meat mix with onions and tomatoes and take it to the nearby bakery. They'd roll out the dough thinner than usual and she would make at least four for each person. We love them served with a squeeze of lemon and a sprinkle of chilli powder and with an ayran yoghurt drink on the side.

A popular Armenian bakery in Zokak El Blat called Ichkhanian Bakery makes their mix with an Aleppo-Armenian twist. Established in 1946, it is still one of the most popular spots among tourists and locals alike. The Armenian-style lahm baajine comes with parsley and warm spices while the pomegranate molasses version is similar to an old-style mince pie with minced meat, warm spices and the sweet and savoury flavour of pomegranate molasses. Here I give four different filling mixtures. Each filling makes enough to top six flatbreads.

MAKES 6

FOR THE BASIC DOUGH

350 g (2⅓ cups) strong (bread) flour or plain (all-purpose) flour, plus extra for dusting

7 g (scant 1 teaspoon) fine salt

200 ml (generous ¾ cup) water

1 teaspoon white granulated sugar

½ teaspoon instant dried yeast

2 tablespoons olive oil

FOR THE LEBANESE FILLING

100 g (3½ oz) tomato

100 g (3½ oz) onion

1 teaspoon fine salt

250 g (9 oz) minced (finely ground) beef (10% fat)

Method and fillings continue overleaf

In a large bowl or a stand mixer fitted with a dough hook, combine all the dough ingredients, except the olive oil, and mix to incorporate until you have a shaggy dough. If you're using a stand mixer, run until the dough comes together into a ball and cleans the sides of the bowl. If kneading by hand, take out of the bowl onto the work surface and knead until a ball forms and it's no longer very sticky. Coat the inside of the mixing bowl with the olive oil, turn the ball of dough in it to coat and cover with cling film (plastic wrap). Set aside to rest for at least 20 minutes.

Take the dough out and divide it into 6 pieces. Roll each piece into a ball, then set aside, covered with cling film or a damp dish towel.

Preheat the oven to the highest temperature (250°C/500°F/gas 10, more if possible) and place a pizza stone or a baking sheet on the middle shelf to heat up. Alternatively, heat a heavy frying pan on the stove to cook the dough in.

Lahm Baajine cont.

FOR THE ARMENIAN FILLING

100 g (3½ oz) tomato

100 g (3½ oz) onion

50 g (1¾ oz) green or red bell pepper

1 green or red chilli (optional)

1 teaspoon chilli powder

1½ teaspoons fine salt

1 teaspoon paprika

250 g (9 oz) minced (finely ground)
  beef (10% fat)

**FOR THE POMEGRANATE
MOLASSES FILLING**

100 g (3½ oz) onion

1 teaspoon allspice

1 teaspoon ground cinnamon

1 teaspoon salt

1 teaspoon tomato or red pepper
  paste

4 tablespoons pomegranate molasses

250 g (9 oz) minced (finely ground)
  beef (10% fat)

FOR THE VEGAN FILLING

100 g (3½oz) tomato

100 g (3½oz) onion

50 g (1¾ oz) green or red bell pepper

1 green or red chilli (optional)

1 teaspoon chilli powder

1½ teaspoons fine salt

1 teaspoon paprika

250 g (9 oz) white or portobello
  mushrooms, finely chopped or
  blitzed in a food processor

TO SERVE

squeeze of lemon juice

sprinkle of chilli powder

To prepare the fillings: In the bowl of a food processor, pulse the vegetables and seasonings until finely blended. Transfer to a bowl and add the meat (or mushrooms) and mix with your hands until well combined. Set aside to rest for 10 minutes. Mix slightly with a spoon before scooping on top of the dough.

On a well-floured surface, use a rolling pin to roll out each ball of dough as thinly as possible (2–3 mm/⅛ in). Transfer to a wooden board. Spread 2 tablespoons of your chosen filling onto the dough and transfer to the hot stone or baking sheet in the oven (or the frying pan on the stovetop) and cook until the toppings are cooked through and the edges of the dough have crisped up.

Remove from the oven or frying pan, place in a high-sided tray and cover with a clean dish towel to let them cool, or serve immediately with a squeeze of lemon juice and a sprinkle of chilli powder. You can also fold them in half, cool and store them in the refrigerator (for up to 2 days) or in the freezer (up to 2 weeks).

Savoury Snacks

One could argue that making a full meal out of appetisers – or what we call mezze – can be fulfilling and delicious. There is so much variety to choose from in Lebanon, one can easily fill a lunch or dinner table with a dip, a salad and a few small plates of these recipes and not feel the need for a main dish. This is often what we order when eating out at Lebanese restaurants.

Most of these recipes can be prepared ahead of time and stored in the freezer until needed, and then can be reheated from frozen in the deep-fryer or oven in mere minutes. This makes them extremely practical, even if some can be a little time-consuming to prepare. The fact that they can be stored for weeks makes the few hours of work worthwhile.

A Lebanese meal will start with the familiar cold appetisers: hummus, baba ghannouj, labneh, white cheese, stuffed vine leaves and some seasonal salads. This is followed by platters of hot appetisers. What you can expect is a couple of *rqaqat jebne* (page 66), *sambousik* meat pastries (page 82), *kibbeh* balls (pages 67 and 70), and *fatayer* (pages 81–87). But the list can go on and on with different specialties and variations on the classics that are commonly found in homes and on restaurant menus.

We would get dozens of these savoury appetisers on cardboard trays in paper bags from the bakery for different occasions: for work meetings, birthdays (serving them before the cake and other sweets), for a breakfast *subhiye* (coffee morning) or afternoon *asrouniye* (teatime gathering), or for funerals. We would usually get mini za'atar *manouche* or ones with cheese (page 46 and 48), mini *lahm baajine* (page 56), *fatayer* triangles filled with spinach or seasonal greens, and some cheese parcels. Even mini pizzas made it to the list (not traditional – we would make our own with tomato sauce or ketchup, sliced deli ham or turkey, black olives, green peppers and cheese... Italians would be furious).

Try making a collection of these recipes and storing them in the freezer until you need them for a quick-to-put-together and luscious spread that will definitely impress. Alternatively, *fatayer* (page 81) can make a perfect side to a winter soup for a filling meal; while *rqaqat* (page 64 and 66) and *kibbeh* go well with hummus and tabbouleh for a light meal.

Rqaqat Ardi Shawki w Sbanekh

Artichoke and spinach rolls

I follow my mom's example here and make a large batch of this recipe to use when I'm in need of a quick fix or some party finger food. The filling is my personal take on an artichoke and spinach dip and it makes a perfect bite-sized snack. Fried until crisp and golden, these have the ideal combination of crispness from the pastry and creaminess and gooey stretchiness from the cheesy filling.

In a food processor, blitz the artichokes with the garlic and salt until chopped to 5 mm (¼ in) chunks or a little smaller.

In a deep frying pan, heat the olive oil and cook the artichoke and garlic mix until fragrant. Add the spinach and stir until all the liquid has evaporated, then set aside to cool.

Once cooled, add the labneh, cheese/s and red pepper flakes and mix to combine.

To assemble, lay a spring roll wrapper with one of the pointy edges facing you. Place 2 tablespoons, around 40 g (1½ oz), of filling in the corner closest to you, fold the pointy edge over the filling, then fold the sides in to seal in the filling. Roll the dough until a small triangle remains. Brush a little bit of water, or water with mixed with a little flour, on the triangle to help seal and roll all the way up. Repeat to fill the remaining rolls. Arrange on a tray in a single layer and freeze until solid. They will keep frozen for up to 2 months in a sealed container.

To bake, take out of the freezer and brush all sides with olive oil. Arrange on a baking sheet and either bake for 20 minutes in a 200°C (400°F/gas 6) oven, or cook in an air fryer at the same temperature, until golden.

To deep fry, heat a 5 cm (2 in) depth of vegetable oil in a deep frying pan until hot. Drop the rolls straight from the freezer into the oil and fry until golden, flipping as needed. Remove with a slotted spoon to drain on kitchen paper.

Serve immediately.

MAKES 20

250 g (9 oz) frozen artichoke bottoms, defrosted

25 g (1 oz) garlic cloves

1½ teaspoons salt

60 ml (¼ cup) olive oil

400 g (14 oz) frozen chopped spinach, defrosted

100 g (3½ oz) thick labneh

300 g (2 cups) grated mozzarella

100 g (⅔ cup) grated desalinated Czech Akkawi cheese (or queso fresco or more mozzarella)

2 teaspoons red pepper flakes

20 spring roll wrappers (I use square ones)

olive oil (for baking or air-frying) or vegetable oil (for deep-frying)

Rqaqat Jebne

Cheese rolls

A plate of hot mezze is never complete without rqaqat jebne, *cheese rolls that are golden and crispy with a soft, stretchy cheese filling. My mom usually makes a large batch and freezes them (they need to be frozen to prevent the cheese from oozing out when cooking) and takes out a dozen to fry when we have people over.*

300 g (10½ oz) Czech Akkawi cheese
200 g (7 oz) mozzarella cheese
100 g (3½ oz) onion
5 sprigs of flat-leaf parsley
3 tablespoons dried mint (optional)
400 g (14 oz) spring roll wrappers
vegetable oil, for brushing or
  for deep-frying

NOTE

In this recipe I have added no extra salt other than that you get from the cheese, so if not using Akkawi, adjust the saltiness to your liking.

Shred the Akkawi cheese and rinse it twice in clean water to remove the excess salt. Taste to check whether a third rinse is needed.

Grate the mozzarella and onion and mix together with the Akkawi. Chop the parsley and add it along with the dried mint, if using. Mix until incorporated.

To assemble, lay a spring roll wrapper with one of the pointy edges facing you. Fold the corner closest to you until the tip reaches the centre of the square. Add around 2 tablespoons of the filling mixture on top of the folded area. Fold in the right and left corners (they will slightly cover the filling) and begin to roll away from you. Make sure that the roll is not too loose. Wet your fingers with a little bit of water and dampen the top corner and roll to seal. Place on a baking sheet and repeat until all the filling is used up.

Freeze the rolls at least for 2 hours before cooking.

When ready to serve, take the rolls out of the freezer and deep-fry in hot oil for around 4 minutes, turning as needed until they're golden all over.

Alternatively, you can bake these. Brush with oil on the baking sheet and bake at 200°C (400°F/gas 6) for 12–15 minutes until golden.

Muhammara Kibbeh

Burghul wheat balls stuffed with pepper paste

MAKES 20 PIECES

FOR THE MUHAMMARA

2 red bell peppers, around 350 g
   (12½ oz)

100 g (3½ oz) walnuts
   (optionally toasted)

2 tablespoons olive oil

3 tablespoons pomegranate molasses

50 g (1¾ oz) red pepper paste (sweet
   or spicy)

1 tablespoon Aleppo pepper

1 tablespoon paprika

2 teaspoons salt

½ teaspoon ground cumin

FOR THE KIBBEH

175 g (1 cup) fine burghul

200 ml (generous ¾ cup) water

100 g (3½ oz) onion

1 teaspoon salt

2 tablespoons Lebanese 7-spice blend

300 g (10½ oz) finely minced (ground)
   beef (or 60 g/generous ⅓ cup plain/
   all-purpose flour for a vegan version)

vegetable or olive oil, for greasing

yoghurt, to serve

~~~~~~~~

method continues overleaf

A staple in the hot mezze selection of any Lebanese table, kibbeh can be made with so many variations and different fillings and sauces (I could write a whole chapter about kibbeh). This recipe is inspired by a Lebanese-Armenian restaurant in Beirut that I go to. Muhammara is a dip that comes from the Syrian and Aleppo-Armenian cuisine made of roasted red bell peppers. Filling the kibbeh with this dip makes a great change from the classic meat filling.

The muhammara recipe makes more than double what you need to use here, but it has so many other uses – use to top Tartine Toasts (page 92) or as a dip. To make this vegan, omit the beef and add flour to the kibbeh mixture to help it bind instead.

For the *muhammara*, char all the sides of the red peppers directly on the flames of the stovetop or under the grill (broiler). (Alternatively, place in a roasting tray, cover with kitchen foil and roast until soft, but they won't have the smoky flavour.) Place in a bowl and cover with cling film (plastic wrap). Set aside for at least 20 minutes to steam.

Peel the blackened skin away from the peppers and wash to remove any remaining blackened bits. Dry with kitchen paper, then slice open, deseed and place in a food processor with the walnuts. Process until smooth, then add the rest of the muhammara ingredients and blend until smooth. (It it is still runny, you can add breadcrumbs to soak up excess moisture.) Store in an airtight container in the refrigerator.

For the *kibbeh*, soak the burghul in the water for around 5 minutes, ensuring it is completely covered. Drain any excess water after this time.

In a food processor, combine the drained burghul with the onion, salt and spice blend. Pulse until the onion is incorporated, then add the beef and process until smooth. Cover and refrigerate the mixture if it is starting to become warm.

Muhammara Kibbeh cont.

(If making the vegan version, pulse the same ingredients, except the beef, until incorporated, then place in a bowl and gradually add the flour until the mix comes together.)

Preheat the oven to 180°C (350°F/gas 4).

Have some iced water in a small wide bowl nearby. Wet your hands and take a piece of the kibbeh mix that is the size of a ping pong ball. Roll into a ball, then push your index finger into the ball. Applying a little pressure, rotate the ball to make a hole and thin out the sides. Alternatively, you can flatten the mixture completely into a disc with your palms. Take a teaspoon of the *muhammara* and drop it into the hole, then pinch to close. Roll into a ball or pinch the sides into a rugby ball shape. If you flattened the mix, fold it slightly in half to contain the filling and pinch it like an empanada. Place on a greased baking sheet and repeat until you have used up all the *kibbeh* mixture. Brush the tops with vegetable or olive oil.

Bake in the oven for 15 minutes, or until browned and crispy.

You can also freeze the unbaked *kibbeh* in a single layer on a tray, then store in a sealed container for up to 2 months. Bake or fry immediately out of the freezer.

Serve with salad and yoghurt for dipping.

Kibbet Samak

Fish *kibbeh*

I tried this fish kibbeh *at a seafood restaurant in Batroun, North Lebanon, called Al Jammal. The experience of eating there is enviable, if you're able to book one of the most sought-after tables – one pressed into the pebbles of the shore, where every diner has their feet tickled by the ebb and flow of the Mediterranean Sea. It's truly a lush experience – and so is the food there, from raw fish and shrimp to Lebanese classics and some chef's creations. The fish* kibbeh *bites were something new for me to try, since the only* kibbeh *we tend to make at home are the meat or pumpkin versions, or meatless burghul balls for Lent stews. For this recipe I decided to go all out on seafood and fill the* kibbeh *with shrimp, but it can be omitted, in which case add more onions instead.*

MAKES 20–22 PIECES

300 g (1¾ cups) fine burghul
400 g (14 oz) white fish fillets
  (fresh or frozen)
50 g (1¾ oz) onion
zests from 1 lemon and 1 orange
10 g (¼ oz) coriander (cilantro)
1 teaspoon salt
1 teaspoon ground cumin
1 teaspoon ground ginger

FOR THE FILLING

200 g (7 oz) onion
1 tablespoon olive oil
400 g (14 oz) cooked baby shrimp
  (a little more if using raw)
20 g (¾ oz) coriander (cilantro),
  finely chopped
1 garlic clove, minced
1 teaspoon salt
1 tablespoon sumac

FOR THE SAUCE

60 ml (¼ cup) lemon juice
1 garlic clove, minced
1 tablespoon sumac
1 tablespoon pomegranate molasses
  (optional)

Soak the burghul in cold water for around 15 minutes, ensuring it is completely covered.

Dry the fish with kitchen paper. (I tend to use frozen fillets, so defrost them first, strain in a colander, then squeeze out the excess liquid.) Place in a food processor along with the onion, lemon and orange zests, coriander, salt, cumin and ginger. Pulse until smooth. Add the burghul, draining the excess liquid if there is any left, and process for a minute or two until the mix is smooth. The burghul might not be crushed completely, but try to get it as smooth as possible to make a dough. (Alternatively, you could run the wet burghul through a meat grinder). Cover the mix and refrigerate for 20 minutes.

For the filling, finely chop the onion (I like to run it in the food processor as well for a finer texture). Heat the olive oil in a small saucepan over a medium to medium-low heat, add the onions and sauté until all the liquid evaporates without burning the onions.

Roughly chop the baby shrimp with a knife or in the food processor and add to the onions along with the coriander, garlic, salt and sumac. Cook for 30 seconds, then remove from the heat and strain to remove any excess liquid (stuffing the *kibbeh* with a wet filling might affect the structure of the *kibbeh* shell).

Have some iced water in a small wide bowl nearby. Wet your hands and take a piece of the *kibbeh* mix that is the size of a ping pong ball. Roll into a ball, then push your index finger into the ball. Applying gentle pressure, rotate the ball in your palm to make a hole and thin out the sides. Alternatively, you can flatten the mixture completely into a disc with your palms. Take 1 teaspoon of the filling and drop it into the hole, then pinch to close. Add more filling if the

hollowed part needs more, but don't overstuff it. Form the stuffed ball into the shape of a rugby ball with slightly pointed ends. If you flattened the mix, fold it over itself to contain the filling, then roll it into a ball and shape as above. Set aside and repeat until the *kibbeh* and filling are used up.

You can refrigerate or freeze the *kibbeh*, or cook them immediately. To cook, deep-fry them in hot oil for 3–4 minutes until golden brown, then drain on kitchen paper. If I know I won't be eating them all that day, I like to fry the extra ones just until they start to get a little colour, then refrigerate or freeze them at that point. To reheat, bake them in a 180°C (350°F/gas 4) oven for 8 minutes if refrigerated, or 10–12 minutes if frozen, until crispy on the outside and hot all the way through.

In a small bowl, mix together the sauce ingredients and serve alongside the *kibbeh*.

Crispy Tuna Rice Bites

This recipe came about by accident. At first I was testing out versions of rice kibbeh, an Iraqi speciality with minced (ground) meat filling that has cousins all over the world. But while researching, I thought of making it like those crispy rice bites that trended online not long ago, with a filling of trout or fresh tuna. At first I intended to get some local fish from a small supplier, but they couldn't get me any that could be consumed raw, so I resorted to using a jar of Mediterranean tuna in olive oil called Balamida (Bonito) and turned this into a tropical version of a canapé, with homemade mayo, avocado and mango cubes and some fresh herbs.

Soak the rice in water for 30 minutes, then drain and rinse.

Place the soaked rice in a large saucepan with the measured water and bring to the boil. Reduce the heat, cover and cook for 15–20 minutes until the water is absorbed. Keep the lid on and let it sit for 5 minutes.

Mash the cooked rice with a potato masher or in a stand mixer fitted with a dough hook until it starts to become dough-like. Allow it to cool before shaping.

Prepare the filling by flaking the tuna into a bowl, then mixing it with the mayo, avocado and mango. Mix in the ginger and garlic and season with salt and lemon juice, to taste.

To shape the rice I would suggest you press it into a tray lined with oiled cling film (plastic wrap), leave it to cool completely, then cut into rectangles with a greased knife. Do not fill with the filling if using this method.

Alternatively, you can shape it with wet hands into balls just larger than a ping pong ball and core them with your finger. Fill with a teaspoon of the filling and close them. If coring is hard, press the rice into a flat disc, fill and fold over to close.

Heat the oil in a frying pan until hot, then fry the rice balls or the rice rectangles until crispy on all sides. If using the rectangle method, top the fried pieces with the tuna filling. Sprinkle with the coriander leaves and serve.

MAKES 10–12 PIECES

250 g (1 cup plus 2 tablespoons) short-grain rice

600 ml (20½ fl oz) water

1 x 185 g (6½ oz) can of tuna (120–125 g/3½–4½ oz drained)

40 g (scant 3 tablespoons) mayonnaise

40 g (1½ oz) avocado, cubed

40 g (1½ oz) mango, cubed

small knob of fresh root ginger, grated

1 garlic clove, grated

½ teaspoon salt (or to taste)

1 tablespoon lemon juice (or to taste)

60–120 ml (¼–½ cup) vegetable oil, for frying

about 10 sprigs of coriander (cilantro), leaves picked, to serve

Sfeeha Baalbekiye

Open-topped meat pies from Baalbek

These small bites are a version of the open-topped meat pies that are commonly made in Baalbek and are known as sfeeha Baalbekiye, *although they are made all over Lebanon. The best bakery in Baalbek to get* sfeeha *is called Lakkis (they have other branches around the country, even in Beirut). For a more rustic experience, go to the small souk close to the Baalbek ruins site and do it like the locals: ask the butcher for meat for* sfeeha, *watch him prepare it in front of your eyes, take it to the bakery right next to or in front of it, where they will bake it, and you can eat it on the spot as soon as it comes out of the oven.*

The sfeeha in Tripoli are similar to arayes, *a mix of spiced meat, onions and tomatoes baked in a pita bread.*

MAKES 40 SMALL PIES

250 g (1⅔ cups) plain (all-purpose) flour, plus extra for dusting
¼ teaspoon instant dried yeast
½ teaspoon white granulated sugar
½ teaspoon salt
70 ml (¼ cup plus 2 teaspoons) olive oil, plus extra for brushing
175 ml (generous ⅔ cup) water

FOR THE FILLING
1 small onion (120 g/4½ oz)
1 tomato (170 g/6 oz)
250 g (9 oz) finely minced (ground) beef (around 10% fat)
2 tablespoons red pepper paste
1 teaspoon salt
1 tablespoon Lebanese 7-spice blend
1 tablespoon pomegranate molasses

TO SERVE
pomegranate molasses
chopped fresh veggies
lemon wedges
red pepper paste (or a sprinkling of your red pepper powder of choice)
ayran yoghurt drink

Make the dough by combining the flour, yeast, sugar and salt in a large bowl. Add the oil and water and mix until a dough comes together. It is a rather wet dough. Turn out onto the work surface and knead for 5–7 minutes until elastic. Coat the dough in a little olive oil and return to the bowl, cover with a plastic bag and leave to rest for 30–45 minutes until doubled in size.

Prepare the filling by pulsing the onion and tomato in a food processor until smooth. Add the beef, pepper paste, salt, 7-spice and pomegranate molasses and pulse again until incorporated.

Preheat the oven to 200°C (400°F/gas 6).

Once the dough has rested, turn out onto a floured or oiled work surface and divide into 4 pieces. Return 3 pieces to the bowl and cover them. Divide the remaining piece into 10 equal pieces and roughly roll them into balls. Flatten each ball into a disc with the heel of your hand. Place 1 teaspoon of the filling mixture in the centre of each disc and slightly lift and pinch 2 opposite sides of each disc to create a shape resembling a boat cradling the filling. Repeat, pinching the opposite sides to form a square with 4 raised and pinched sides.

Arrange on a baking sheet and bake for 15–17 minutes until browned. (Depending on the size of your baking sheets, you may need to form and bake these in batches.)

Serve immediately with pomegranate molasses, veggies, lemon wedges, red pepper paste or powder and a glass of *ayran* yoghurt drink on the side.

Store leftovers in a sealed container and refrigerate for up to 5 days, or freeze for up to 2 months.

Souborek

Layered cheese pie

A classic Aleppo-Armenian appetiser that is usually shared. These are typically made of fresh silky egg noodle sheets that are boiled and layered with a cheese mix and parsley, then topped with butter before baking. Ickhanian, an Armenian bakery in Zokak El Blat in Beirut, used to have a freezer filled with trays of shish barak, mante and souborek ready to be baked and delivered, or delivered frozen.

I make a shortcut version that uses ready-made filo pastry sheets to create the crispy edges I like in a souborek. As for the layering, I prefer to have alternating layers of dough and filling, but you can definitely make it into a pie and have all the filling in one layer. This recipe freezes well and can be baked when needed.

Rinse the grated Akkawi cheese in cold water to remove most of the salt. Mix it in a bowl with the mozzarella and feta, then add the eggs and chopped parsley and mix until incorporated.

Brush the base of a 25 cm (10 in) square baking tray (or equivalent) with melted butter, then lay 3 filo sheets in the pan, letting some of the sheets overhang the sides of the pan. Brush with more butter.

Add a third of the cheese mix in an even layer, then top with another 3 filo sheets. Brush with butter and top with another third of the cheese mix. Repeat with another layer of sheets, brushing with butter, then add the final portion of cheese mix.

Top the last 3 filo sheets, one at a time, brushing each one with butter before adding the next. Tuck all the sheets well inside the edges of the pan.

Refrigerate for at least 2 hours, or freeze before baking.

Bake in a 200°C (400°F/gas 6) oven for 25–30 minutes until golden.

Cut into portions and serve immediately.

MAKES 9 PORTIONS

250 g (9 oz) Czech Akkawi cheese, grated
250 g (9 oz) mozzarella cheese, grated
100 g (3½ oz) feta cheese, crumbled
2 eggs
40 g (1½ oz) parsley, finely chopped
80 g (2¾ oz) butter, melted
250 g (9 oz) filo (phyllo) pastry sheets (around 12 sheets)

Borek Soujok w Jebne

Spicy sausage and cheese pies

MAKES AROUND 24 PASTRIES

vegetable oil, for deep-frying

FOR THE DOUGH

250 g (1⅔ cups) plain (all-purpose)
  flour, plus (optional) extra for dusting

2 tablespoons olive oil

¾ teaspoon salt

1 teaspoon white granulated sugar

150 ml (scant ⅔ cup) water (or milk)

FOR THE FILLING

200 g (7 oz) *soujok* (available in
  Middle-Eastern stores)
  OR
  10 g (¼ oz) *soujok* spices (see below)
  2 garlic cloves, minced
  1 tablespoon red pepper paste
  200 g (7 oz) finely minced
    (ground) beef

150 g (5 oz) Czech Akkawi cheese

150 g (5 oz) mozzarella cheese

25 g (1 oz) onion, finely chopped

small handful of flat-leaf parsley,
  finely chopped

FOR THE *SOUJOK* SPICE MIX
  (OPTIONAL, IF NOT USING *SOUJOK*)

½ teaspoon allspice

1½ teaspoons ground white pepper

1 teaspoon ground black pepper

1 tablespoon ground cumin

2 teaspoons salt

¼ teaspoon ground nutmeg

1½ tablespoons garlic powder

1½ tablespoons paprika

1½ tablespoons dried chilli
  (red pepper) flakes

1½ tablespoons ground fenugreek

Soujok (an Armenian spicy sausage) can be found in butcher shops all over Lebanon, but is known to be made best by Armenians. I tasted these soujok and cheese borek in Mayrig, a well-known Armenian restaurant in Beirut and tried to recreate them. You can adjust the shape to your liking, but this is how they make them.

Ready-made soujok can be used in this recipe. If not available, mix soujok spices, garlic and red pepper paste with minced (ground) beef until well incorporated. The spice mix makes more than you will need, but store in an airtight container for when you need it next.

In a large bowl, mix all the ingredients for the dough and knead for 5 minutes until a smooth dough is formed. Cover and rest for 30 minutes.

For the filling, if not using ready-made *soujok*, mix the *soujok* spices, garlic and red pepper paste with the beef until incorporated. Cover and set aside for at least 30 minutes, or refrigerate to use later. The more it marinates, the better.

Shred the Akkawi cheese, rinse it twice in clean water and check to make sure it's not too salty. Mix it with the mozzarella, onion and parsley, then add the *soujok* or spiced beef and mix until incorporated.

The dough should not be very sticky, but if it is, add a little bit of flour to the work surface. Take a third or quarter of the dough (based on how comfortable you are and how big your work surface is) and roll it out to 2 mm (¹⁄₁₆ in) thick, then cut into 5 cm (2 in) squares. Fill each square with a teaspoon of the filling mixture, then bring the opposite sides of each square together and pinch to close at the top. Using a fork, press the top and bottom part of each pastry to close it. Repeat the process with the remaining dough and filling.

If there are parts of the dough that were unused when cut out and returned to the dough in the bowl, make sure to give them enough time to rest between each roll, otherwise the dough will start to retract and will be hard to roll thin.

Deep-fry in hot oil until golden. Remove with a slotted spoon to drain on kitchen paper and serve immediately.

The pastries can be frozen on a baking sheet until solid, then packed in bags or containers, or can be half-fried, then frozen. They will keep for up to 2 months and can be baked or fried in hot oil straight from the freezer.

Serve immediately.

They will keep frozen for up to 2 months in a sealed container.

Fatayer Zaytoun w Jebne

Olive and cheese parcels

There is something so heavenly about the flavour of cheese with olives, whether it's in a manouche *wrap, in fatayer baked pies, or in fried parcels as here. This is a versatile appetiser recipe: you can try adding sumac, or oregano or basil, maybe tarragon if it's available. Any of these combinations would pair so well with a small saucer of marinara sauce for dipping (and it's better if it's spicy). I use green olives for these as I prefer their flavour, but feel free to substitute black olives or use a mixture of both to suit your taste.*

In a large bowl, mix all the ingredients for the dough and knead for 5 minutes until a smooth dough is formed. Cover and rest for 30 minutes.

Shred the Akkawi cheese and rinse it twice to make sure it is not salty anymore. Mix it with the mozzarella (you can use other types of cheese, but the mozzarella and Akkawi are great for a cheese pull!). Add the chopped olives and spring onions and mix well.

Take out a quarter portion of the dough (cover the rest while you work with it) and roll it out to 2 mm (1/16 in) thick. The dough should not be very sticky, but if needed a little bit of flour could be used. Cut the dough into 7 cm (2¾ in) circles using a cookie cutter or the opening of a glass cup. You could also cut it into squares. Remove the excess dough and store with the remaining dough in the bowl, but I advise using the unused dough last as the dough needs to rest in between rolls.

Place 1 teaspoon of the filling mixture into the middle of each piece of dough. If you cut the dough into circles, bring 2 sides of the disc together around the filling and pinch in the middle. Pinch down one side of the seam to close (leaving the other side open). Bring the dough up from the centre of the open side to meet the middle of the seam, then pinch along the whole length to close completely. The resulting pie should look like a rough pyramid. If you cut the dough into squares, repeat the same process but bring in 2 corners at a time, then pinch the open parts shut, creating a pyramid.

Deep-fry in hot oil until golden. Remove with a slotted spoon to drain on kitchen paper and serve immediately.

The raw pastries can be frozen on a baking sheet, then stored in containers or bags in the freezer for up to 2 months. They can be baked or fried straight from the freezer when needed.

MAKES AROUND 24 PASTRIES

vegetable oil, for deep-frying

FOR THE DOUGH

250 g (1⅔ cups) plain (all-purpose) flour, plus (optional) extra for dusting

2 tablespoons olive oil

¾ teaspoon salt

1 teaspoon white granulated sugar

150 ml (scant ⅔ cup) water (or milk)

FOR THE FILLING

150 g (5 oz) Czech Akkawi cheese

150 g (5 oz) mozzarella cheese, shredded

50 g (1¾ oz) green olives, finely chopped

4 spring onions (scallions), finely chopped

Sambousik Lahme/Jebne

Meat or cheese hand pies

Another classic hot appetiser, sambousik is one of many pastries of similar shape and name. Filled with minced (ground) meat and onions, the toughest part of making them is pinching them shut with a unique braid intricately formed with the tips of the fingers. Of course, they can be crimped like empanada or sealed with a fork, but the beauty of them is in those small twists of dough. The uncooked pastries freeze well and can be fried immediately from frozen – this is why the recipe makes so many, as you'll always want some to hand.

MAKES 24 SMALL PIES OF
EACH FILLING

vegetable oil for deep-frying,
  or olive oil for coating if baking

FOR THE DOUGH
500 g (3⅓ cups) plain (all-
  purpose) flour
4 tablespoons olive oil
10 g (generous 1½ teaspoons) salt
300 ml (scant 1¼ cups) milk

FOR THE MEAT FILLING
200 g (7 oz) minced (ground) beef
200 g (7 oz) onion, finely chopped
1 teaspoon salt
1 teaspoon Lebanese 7-spice blend
2 tablespoons olive oil

FOR THE CHEESE FILLING
100 g (3½ oz) Czech Akkawi cheese,
  soaked in 2 changes of water,
  then grated
100 g (3½ oz) mozzarella cheese,
  grated
50 g (1¾ oz) feta cheese
50 g (1¾ oz) labneh (or sour cream)
50 g (1¾ oz) onion, grated
2 tablespoons chopped flat-leaf
  parsley

In a large bowl or a stand mixer fitted with a dough hook, combine the flour, 3 tablespoons of the olive oil, the salt and milk and mix until you have a shaggy dough. If using a stand mixer, run until the dough comes together into a ball and cleans the sides of the bowl. If kneading by hand, transfer to the work surface and knead until a ball forms and it's no longer sticky. Coat the inside of the bowl with the remaining oil, turn the ball of dough in it to coat and cover with cling film (plastic wrap). Leave to rest for at least 20 minutes.

Grab a baseball-sized piece of dough and roll it on the work surface (no need for extra flour) to a thickness of 5 mm (¼ in). Using a cutter or the rim of a cup, cut the dough into circles, 6–7 cm (2¾ in) in diameter. Return the scraps to the covered bowl with the rest of the dough.

For the fillings, simply mix all the ingredients for each filling in a separate bowl until well combined.

Fill each circle of dough with a teaspoon of the filling, fold it in half in a half-moon shape and pinch it shut. To shape it, you can use a fork to crimp the edges like empanadas, but the method I learned from my mom is a bit more intricate. After pinching it, thin out the edges. Starting from the top of the crescent, fold what's between your thumb and forefinger onto the next piece of dough along the crescent and pinch, then take this part and repeat until all of the side is braided like a Cornish pasty. Arrange on a tray without them touching while you make the rest.

If deep-frying, fry in hot oil until golden, turning as needed. Drain on kitchen paper.

If baking, generously brush all sides with olive oil, place on a baking sheet and bake in a 200°C (400°F/gas 6) oven for 12–15 minutes until golden.

Freeze any uncooked pies in a single layer until solid, then store in an airtight container in the freezer for up to 4 months. Cook straight from the freezer in hot frying oil until golden or bake as above.

Fatayer Batata

Potato parcels

Fatayer means "pies", it's a catch-all term for any turnover or hand-pie, mostly in the shape of a triangle with countless fillings. I got this recipe from my friend Hanine, who learned it from her family in the Bekaa. Even with simple ingredients, it packs in bold flavours from the dried mint and the fatty awarma (lamb confit). Hanine always brought me a small pack of awarma that her mom used to make up before she passed away. She took pride in her mom's awarma and she had every right to – it was delicious. To make this recipe, Hanine and I asked her relatives to give us their version and I tried what felt would work for me. What I love about this is the crumbly texture of the filling with the potatoes still holding their shape even after cooking and the burst of flavour from the awarma and dried mint.

MAKES 16 PASTRIES

FOR THE DOUGH

250 g (1⅔ cups) plain (all-purpose) flour

¼ teaspoon instant dried yeast

½ teaspoon white granulated sugar

½ teaspoon salt

70 ml (¼ cup plus 2 teaspoons) olive oil, plus extra for brushing

175 ml (generous ⅔ cup) water

FOR THE FILLING

1 kg (2 lb 4 oz) potatoes, peeled and grated

250 g (9 oz) onions, grated

1 tablespoon salt, plus 1 teaspoon if the *awarma* is not very salty

100 g (3½ oz) *awarma* (lamb confit – buy in Middle Eastern delis or online; or see page 52 for substitutes)

8 g (1½ tablespoons) dried mint

½ teaspoon citric acid

4 tablespoons olive oil

Make the dough by combining the flour, yeast, sugar and salt in a large bowl. Add the oil and water and mix until a dough comes together. It is a rather wet dough. Knead for 5–7 minutes until elastic. Coat in a little bit of olive oil and return to the bowl and cover with a bag or plastic bag and let it rest and prove for 30–45 minutes until doubled in size.

Prepare the filling by adding the grated potatoes and onions to a large bowl. Add 1 tablespoon of the salt, mix well and leave to sit for 15 minutes.

Strain and squeeze out the excess liquid from the potatoes and onions (a muslin/cheesecloth helps with this), then mix in the *awarma*, dried mint, citric acid and olive oil, plus the teaspoon of salt (if needed).

Preheat the oven to 200°C (400°F/gas 6).

Once the dough has rested, turn out onto the work surface and divide into 4 pieces. Return 3 pieces to the bowl and cover them. Divide the remaining piece into 4 equal pieces and roll each into a ball. Flatten each ball using the heel of your hand or a rolling pin to an 8 cm (3¼ in) disc. Fill each disc with a heaped tablespoon of the filling, then bring 2 sides of the disc together around the filling and pinch in the middle. Pinch down one side of the seam to close (leaving the other side open). Bring the dough up from the centre of the open side to meet the middle of the seam, then pinch along the whole length to close completely. The resulting pie should look like a rough pyramid shape. Repeat to use up the remaining dough and filling mixture.

Arrange on an oiled baking sheet and brush the pastries with more oil. Bake for 30 minutes until golden.

Fatayer Mhammar

Mhammar hand pies

Mhammar *is a traditional Palestinian traybake of chicken pieces with potato wedges and a sauce of onions and red bell peppers, slow-cooked in the oven until tender. I wanted to improvise a little on the recipe and make it more portable than a saucy tray that needs to be scooped up with bread. The puff pastry in these hand pies contrasts beautifully with the soft filling and it still reminds me of the original dish.*

Massage the salt into the grated potatoes and set aside for 10 minutes. Strain though muslin (cheesecloth) until the excess water is removed. Set aside.

Over a flame on the hob or under the grill (broiler), char the peppers until a black film coats the outside. Place in a bowl or bag and seal completely to steam for 15 minutes. This will make peeling easier. Uncover and peel, then remove and discard the seeds and rinse the flesh if needed to remove any charred skin residue.

In a food processor, pulse the pepper flesh with the onion until finely chopped.

Finely chop the chicken breast into tiny cubes or quickly pulse in a food processor. Add the pepper paste and spices and mix well.

Heat half of the olive oil in a deep saucepan over a medium heat and fry the chicken mixture until lightly browned. Add the pepper and onion mixture along with the grated potatoes and stir for about 10 minutes until the vegetables have softened. (Add 2–4 tablespoons of water if the mixture is too dry and the vegetables are still too raw.) Set aside to cool.

Preheat the oven to 200°C (400°F/gas 6).

If using block pastry, roll out each block to a 50 x 20 cm (20 x 8 in) rectangle, then cut each block into 10 squares, 10 x 10 cm (4 x 4 in) each. If using ready-made 13-cm (5-in) pastry squares, they don't need to be trimmed.

To assemble, lay out your pastry squares and scoop 1½–2 tablespoons of the filling into the middle of each. Take one corner of each square over to the diagonally opposite corner to create a triangle. Lightly press the edges to seal, or press with a fork to create a nice pattern. Brush with vegetable oil and place on a lined baking sheet.

Bake for 10–12 minutes until puffed and golden. Serve immediately.

Store leftovers in a sealed container for up to 3 days. Uncooked pies can be frozen for up to 2 months and baked for 15 minutes straight from the freezer until golden, or fried in hot oil.

MAKES 18–20 PASTRIES

1 tablespoon salt

400 g (14 oz) potatoes, peeled and grated

350 g (12½ oz) red bell peppers

250 g (9 oz) onion, peeled

500 g (1 lb 2 oz) chicken breast (or thighs)

2 tablespoons red pepper paste (or more, if you like a bit of a kick)

1 teaspoon allspice

½ teaspoon ground nutmeg

½ teaspoon ground cinnamon

1 teaspoon each black and white pepper

125 ml (½ cup) olive oil

1 kg (2 lb 4 oz) block of puff pastry (or 18–20 x 13-cm/5-in square sheets, sold pre-cut and frozen in Middle Eastern stores), thawed if frozen

vegetable oil, for brushing

Arayes Msakhan

Palestinian sumac chicken and onion pitas

This is a modern adaptation of an authentic recipe. Msakhan is among the most well-known recipes from Palestinian cuisine. It is traditionally made with taboon bread covered in olive oil, caramelised onions and sumac-seasoned bone-in chicken, all baked until cooked through. My mom's version is made with shredded boiled chicken with the same seasonings but wrapped in saj/ marqouq bread, then baked. My version uses pita bread filled with ground chicken meat with the same seasonings, pan-fried on both sides until golden and crispy. I enjoy it more when I have made the bread myself – it turns out absolutely delicious. Depending on the sourness of your sumac, adjust the quantity to your liking.

MAKES 6–8

60 ml (¼ cup) olive oil

1 kg (2 lb 4 oz) onions, peeled and thinly sliced

750 g (1 lb 11 oz) boneless skinless chicken (breast or thighs) or minced (ground) chicken

2 teaspoons salt

40 g (¼ cup) sumac

6–8 large pita breads

60 ml (¼ cup) pomegranate molasses, to serve

Heat 2–3 tablespoons of the olive oil in a wide frying pan over a medium heat and cook the onions for 20–30 minutes, stirring occasionally to prevent burning, until they start caramelising (reduce the heat even more if needed). Once the onions reach a deep caramel colour, remove from the heat and leave to cool.

If you wish, you can blitz the onions to a purée in a food processor, but they can be used as they are as well.

Process the chicken in a food processor until it's in small pieces. Mix in the caramelised onions, salt and sumac.

Split open the pita breads and fill each with 120–140 g (4½–5 oz) of the filling mixture, depending on the size of your breads. Brush the outsides with the remaining olive oil and grill in a hot dry frying pan for 4–6 minutes on each side until crispy on the outside and cooked through on the inside.

Cut each pita into 4 pieces. Serve drizzled with the pomegranate molasses.

Ouze

Spiced meat and rice parcels

These are a feast in a pie. Ouze is a celebration dish of whole roast lamb served with rice and peas and sometimes carrots. Christmas turkey is also prepared in a similar manner but with seasonal chestnuts as an extra lush ingredient. These parcels are a popular way of repurposing the leftover pulled lamb meat and the rice. Since many of us don't have time to roast a whole lamb, this version uses minced (ground) meat instead. Slow-cooked lamb shanks could also work perfectly. The parcels can be made vegetarian by omitting the meat and by adding a decent amount of spices to a good vegetable broth for cooking the rice.

MAKES 12

2 tablespoons olive oil

300 g (10½ oz) minced (ground) lamb or beef (or a mix of beef and lamb together)

2 tablespoons Lebanese 7-spice blend

2 teaspoons salt

300 g (1½ cups) long-grain rice

700 ml (23½ fl oz) water or beef stock

250 g (1⅔ cups) frozen green peas

50 g (1¾ oz) melted butter (or olive oil)

150 g (1 cup) blanched almonds

25 g (1 oz) filo (phyllo) pastry sheets

TO DECORATE

36 blanched almond halves

TO SERVE

your favourite gravy

OR

pomegranate molasses, for drizzling

NOTE

The parcels, when brushed in butter or oil, can be frozen and baked when needed.

Heat the olive oil in a medium saucepan over a medium-high heat, add the meat, 7-spice and 1 teaspoon of the salt. Sauté until browned. Remove from the pan to a mixing bowl and set aside.

Wash the rice until the water runs clear, then add it to the same pan along with the remaining teaspoon of salt and the water or stock. Bring to the boil, then reduce the heat, cover and cook for around 15 minutes until the water is absorbed and the rice is fully cooked. Fluff the rice and let it sit in the pan for 10 minutes.

Add the rice to the cooked beef, then stir in the frozen peas. This will help cool the rice mix and at the same time defrost the peas.

Heat 30 g (1 oz) of the butter (or 2 tablespoons of oil) in a small pan and fry the almonds until golden and crunchy. Strain off the butter and save, along with the unused portion of butter (or oil). Dry the almonds with kitchen paper.

Preheat the oven to 200°C (400°F/gas 6). Line a baking tray with baking paper.

Cut each pastry sheet into 4 squares, about 13 cm (5 in) each. Take 3 squares of pastry and use them to line a small 7 cm (2¾ in) bowl, making sure that they overlap. Drape the excess pastry over the edge of the bowl. Fill the centre with a tablespoon of the fried almonds and around 130 g (4½ oz) of the rice mix. Bring in the flaps of dough to cover the filling, lightly press and flip over into your hand. Place on the lined baking sheet. Repeat with the rest of the dough and fillings.

Generously brush each pie with the reserved butter (or olive oil), arrange 3 almond halves on top to decorate and bake in the oven for 20–25 minutes until the tops are golden.

Serve immediately for perfect crispiness, with your favourite gravy or some pomegranate molasses.

Tartine Toasts

These are hardly traditional, but instead a creation from ingredients I would usually have at home. I like to make these with sourdough bread, homemade pita bread, or regular toasting bread, browning it in butter or oil. I follow a basic formula: a spread of labneh or whipped feta at the bottom, crunchy vegetables or cheese slices or a fried egg, a sprinkle of spice, a drizzle of oil and some fresh herbs, or a herb or chilli paste. A sweet option might be walnuts and honey with a delicious fig jam. Play around, mix and match, and find a combination that suits your taste. These are a few of the tartines I make the same way over and over again, especially for breakfast.

For each variety of tartine, first toast the bread with a little bit of olive oil or butter in a frying pan over a medium-low heat.

EACH VARIETY SERVES 4

FOR EACH VARIETY

4 pita breads or sourdough slices
olive oil or butter, for toasting

WHIPPED FETA AND BEETROOT

250 g (9 oz) feta cheese
100 g (3½ oz) labneh
olive oil, as needed
1 beetroot (beet), peeled
1 tablespoon white granulated sugar
1 tablespoon salt
1 small red onion, peeled
2 spring onions (scallions)
sea salt flakes (optional)

WHIPPED FETA AND BEETROOT:
In a food processor or with a fork, mash the feta, then add the labneh and 1 tablespoon of olive oil until a chunky mixture is achieved.

Shave the beetroot into ribbons with a vegetable peeler. Soak in iced water with the sugar and salt. Thinly slice the red onion and add it to the water. Thinly slice the spring onions and add to the iced water.

Spread the whipped feta on the toasts. Drain and dry the veggies on kitchen paper, then arrange the beet slices on top, followed by the onions. Season with salt if the feta is not salty enough, drizzle with olive oil and serve.

WHIPPED FETA, ZA'ATAR, TOMATO, CUCUMBER AND LEMON

250 g (9 oz) feta cheese
100 g (3½ oz) labneh
olive oil, as needed
4 tablespoons za'atar
16 cherry or grape tomatoes
1 cucumber
zest of 1 lemon
sea salt flakes

WHIPPED FETA, ZA'ATAR, TOMATO, CUCUMBER AND LEMON:
Use the same whipped feta base as above and spread on each toast. Top each with a tablespoon of za'atar.

Cut the tomatoes in half, lightly salt them, then arrange on top of the toasts. Shave the cucumber into ribbons with a vegetable peeler and arrange on top. Drizzle with olive oil, sprinkle with lemon zest, season with salt and serve.

HUMMUS/MUHAMMARA AND SPICED EGGS

200 g (7 oz) hummus or *muhammara* (page 67)
4 eggs
olive oil or butter, for frying
½ teaspoon ground cinnamon
½ teaspoon ground allspice
sea salt flakes

HUMMUS/MUHAMMARA AND SPICED EGGS:
Divide the hummus or *muhammara* among the toasts.

Fry the eggs, sunny side up, in olive oil and/or butter. Use a spoon to baste the eggs with the hot olive oil. Once they reach your desired doneness, sprinkle with the cinnamon, allspice and salt.

Transfer the eggs to the toasts and serve.

FIG JAM, MOZZARELLA, WALNUT
AND HONEY

6 tablespoons fig jam

16 walnuts

120 g (4½ oz) mozzarella cheese, sliced

honey, for drizzling

GRIDDLED TOMATO, LABNEH,
POMEGRANATE MOLASSES AND MINT

4 roma tomatoes, deseeded and sliced

a drizzle of olive oil

200 g (7 oz) labneh

pomegranate molasses, (or balsamic
glaze), for drizzling

sea salt flakes

mint (or thyme) leaves, to garnish

FIG JAM, MOZZARELLA, WALNUT AND HONEY:

Divide the fig jam among the toasts, sprinkle with the walnuts and top with
the mozzarella.

Transfer to a baking tray and heat in the oven or toast in a dry frying pan until
the cheese has melted.

Drizzle with honey and serve.

GRIDDLED TOMATO, LABNEH, POMEGRANATE MOLASSES AND MINT:

Griddle the tomato slices in a frying pan with a little olive oil.

Divide the labneh among the toasts and top with the griddled tomatoes.
Drizzle with pomegranate molasses, sprinkle with salt, then scatter over the
mint leaves. Drizzle with a little more olive oil and serve.

Pictured overleaf

Crackers for Dips

When I used to make my own sourdough bread at home, I used to have an excess of sourdough starter. I looked up many recipes that would use it up instead of throwing it away. As well as savoury or sweet pancakes, one of the best uses of it is to make crackers. I used to spice them to my liking with za'atar or chilli pepper or make them plain with just salt. To keep things easy I haven't used sourdough starter in this recipe, but if you happen to have some sourdough starter you can definitely adjust the proportions to use it in this recipe. The spices used can also be swapped or adjusted to taste.

EACH RECIPE MAKES AROUND 20 CRACKERS

FOR THE SPICY FLOUR CRACKERS

160 g (generous 1 cup) plain (all-purpose) flour, plus extra for dusting
100 ml (generous ⅓ cup) water
1 teaspoon Aleppo pepper
1 teaspoon salt
1 tablespoon olive oil

FOR THE HERBY CORN CRACKERS

250 g (1⅔ cups) cornmeal
80 ml (⅓ cup) water
1 teaspoon dried oregano
1 teaspoon salt
1 tablespoon olive oil

For each type of cracker, mix all the ingredients in a bowl and knead until a dough comes together (the cornmeal dough will remain crumbly). Cover with cling film (plastic wrap) and rest for 1 hour.

Preheat the oven to 180°C (350°F/gas 4).

For the flour crackers, use a rolling pin to roll out the flour dough with a little flour on baking paper. Roll them as thin as you can. Let them rest for 10 minutes, then cut into 20 pieces with a sharp knife. Transfer the paper to a baking sheet and bake for 7–10 minutes, or until the crackers have dried out. Let the crackers cool before serving.

For the corn crackers, roll the dough out between two pieces of baking paper. Remove the top piece of baking paper and cut into 20 pieces or into triangles. Transfer the paper to a baking sheet and bake for 10–12 minutes, or until the crackers have dried out. Let the crackers cool before serving.

Store in an airtight container for up to 2 weeks.

Bakery
Sweets

In our cities, sweet shops employing a master specialist in their craft are so common that most people will have one close by. As a result, we seldom bother to make traditional sweets at home. The sweet shops and bakeries will always have whatever you crave in stock and they will have made it extremely well. But during this time of upheaval in this part of the world, I feel a responsibility to document and share these recipes to preserve them for the future. Also, I hope they might bring comfort to those living abroad who miss the taste of home and, of course, enlighten those who are curious to try and learn more about our food.

It was tough working on the recipes in this chapter, both practically and emotionally. These are guarded sweet shop secrets. Even if I was lucky enough to get hold of the recipes, some of them required professional skill, experience and sometimes a lot of kitchen space to master properly. I have tried to simplify and demystify the processes to make the recipes both accessible and achievable.

One of the most common ingredients in Lebanese sweets is an element of dairy – milk, butter (or ghee) and cheese. The cheese is usually Akkawi (from Akka in North Palestine) and comes in two versions: regular Akkawi is medium firm and moderately salted, which makes it a great sandwich cheese. The other type, known as Czech Akkawi, is very firm and extra salty, and requires soaking and rinsing multiple times before using in sweets, especially *Knefe* (page 121) and *Halawet el Jeben* (page 124). Mshallale cheese is a form of white string cheese that is shaped into thick braids. It is firm and slightly salty and works for both sandwiches and for sweets such as *Mammouniye* (page 170). Majdoule looks similar to mshallale, but it is not as stringy. Nabulsi cheese (from the Palestinian city of Nablus) is similar to majdoule and halloumi, but is sometimes flavoured with mahlab and contains nigella seeds. It can be pan-fried or melted in a sandwich or used in *Knefe* (page 121). In case any of these cheeses are not available in your local Middle Eastern

stores, mozzarella can replace them in most cases, sometimes with a little bit of feta to add some saltiness, if needed.

Another essential ingredient in most sweets is semolina. Semolina is made from durum wheat, which is a hard type of wheat that is used to make burghul, freekeh and *saj* bread. It comes in *farkha* (fine) and coarse varieties and each one is used for specific recipes. They are not usually interchangeable.

Many recipes use filo pastry sheets and kataifi pastry. While visiting one of my favourite sweet shops for research, I learned that there is a specific type of dough for every type of sweet. The pastry sheets used for *Rqaqat* (page 64 and 66) are different to those used for *baklawa*; the kataifi for rolled *Baklawa Borma* (page 114) is thicker than the one used for *Osmalliye* (page 104) or *Ballouriye* (page 111); *Knafe Nabulsiye* and Lebanese-style *Knefe* both use a slightly differently processed "dough" for the base. But that's a distinction for specialised makers. When I was trying to make the recipes authentically I had to ask for the specific dough from the shop days in advance to get it, but for the sake of easily achievable recipes, I have stuck with the most commonly available pastry options.

You'll notice that *Ashta* (page 102) is common in many recipes. It is typical to buy this from sweet shops to use it in your home recipes. Basic *ashta* is simply the clotted cream repeatedly skimmed off a boiling saucepan of raw milk. This type only works for cold uses, such as filling *Halawet el Jeben*. The more stable version, which can be used in baked and fried recipes, is made by thickening the milk with cornflour (cornstarch) or with semolina, or both, and can be made closer in texture to real *ashta* by adding milk curds or ricotta/cottage cheese.

The last important ingredient is Simple Syrup (page 103). The golden ratio is two parts sugar to one part water for a universal syrup. Flavour it with orange blossom or rose water (or rose geranium, like my mom does), but always add lemon juice or citric acid to prevent the sugar crystallising.

Ashta

Homemade clotted cream

Ashta is the base of many dessert recipes and is the Lebanese version of clotted cream. It is an essential part of Mafrouke (page 126) or Halawet el Jeben (page 124), but is also delicious simply on its own or topped with honey or fruits. Making it can be a hassle, since it requires heating full-fat (whole) milk or cream to the boil, then either leaving it to simmer in a wide baking tray or slow-baking it in a lukewarm oven to develop a fatty layer which is the ashta. It usually takes a long time, but if you have the luxury of time this method makes a superior ashta for use in recipes where the ashta is not heated. For use in recipes that require baking or frying, a thickened milk recipe is needed. I've given a few methods here for different budgets and uses.

MAKES ABOUT 600 G (1 LB 5 OZ)

LONG PROCESS

(FOR USE IN COLD RECIPES)

2 litres (8 cups) full-fat (whole) milk
  (or 1 litre/4 cups milk and
  1 litre/4 cups double/heavy cream)

QUICK PROCESS

(FOR FRYING OR BAKING)

1 litre (4 cups) full-fat (whole) milk
  (or 600 ml/2⅓ cups water with
  250 g/2½ cups milk powder)

30 g (¼ cup) cornflour (cornstarch)

70 g (generous ½ cup) fine semolina

1 teaspoon rose water

1 teaspoon orange blossom water

LUXURIOUS PROCESS

(FOR FRYING OR BAKING)

1 litre (4 cups) full-fat (whole) milk

70 g (generous ½ cup) cornflour
  (cornstarch)

35 g (3 tablespoons) semolina

1 teaspoon rose water

1 teaspoon orange blossom water

250 g (1 cup) cottage cheese or ricotta

LONG PROCESS

Put the milk (or milk and cream) in a large, wide saucepan and bring to the boil. Reduce the heat and let it simmer, uncovered, for 2 hours on the lowest temperature, stirring regularly to prevent burning. Turn off the heat and cover with a clean dish towel or mesh screen and leave undisturbed for 12 hours.

After 12 hours, run a knife through the fat layer that has formed to cut it into thick long strips, around 5 cm (2 in) wide. Carefully remove to a plate, avoiding taking a lot of the remaining milk with it. Pour away any liquid that might have pooled under the *ashta* on the plate. Refrigerate for up to 3 days and use as required in your recipe.

QUICK/LUXURIOUS PROCESS

Mix the milk, cornflour and semolina in a saucepan until incorporated. Place the saucepan over a medium heat and stir the mixture until it comes to the boil and starts to thicken. Remove from the heat and stir in the aromatic waters (and the cheese if making the luxurious version) until incorporated.

Pour the mixture into a container and cover the surface with cling film (plastic wrap) to prevent a skin forming. Allow it to cool to room temperature. Once cooled, break it up with a fork to get a clumpy texture. Store in an airtight container and refrigerate for up to a week.

Simple Syrup

MAKES ABOUT 375 ML (1½ CUPS)

LIGHT SYRUP

250 g (1 cup) white granulated sugar

250 ml (1 cup) water

1 teaspoon lemon juice
  or ¼ teaspoon citric acid

2 teaspoons orange blossom water

2 teaspoons rose water

REGULAR SYRUP

500 g (generous 2 cups) white
  granulated sugar

250 ml (1 cup) water

1 teaspoon lemon juice
  or ¼ teaspoon citric acid

1 tablespoon orange blossom water

1 tablespoon rose water

THICK SYRUP

750 g (generous 3 cups) white
  granulated sugar

250 ml (1 cup) water

1 teaspoon lemon juice
  or ¼ teaspoon citric acid

1 tablespoon orange blossom water

1 tablespoon rose water

Simple syrup is a staple in most of the desserts in this book. The basic dessert recipes tend not to be sweetened (or are just lightly sweetened) so the syrup works to give more control over the sweetness, or acts as a binder and preservative. Each type of syrup has a different use in certain recipes.

Place the sugar in a saucepan, pour over the water and set over a medium heat. Allow the sugar to dissolve completely and bring to the boil undisturbed. Allow it to simmer over a low heat for 5 minutes. Add the lemon juice or citric acid, then remove from heat and add the aromatic waters.

Use as required in your recipe. Leftovers can be stored for later use and can be added to coffee or cocktails, used as a base for lemonade, or drizzled over desserts.

Osmalliye Mess

Osmalliye *reminds me a little of mille-feuille with two layers of baked kataifi pastry crust with a creamy ashta filling. I always find it tedious to eat either dessert with people around, as they both make such a mess. So, I thought why not embrace the mess and make a version inspired by Eton Mess?*

The original recipe can be traced back to the Ottoman Empire. In traditional Arabic, the word Othmani *refers to anything that is Ottoman. In colloquial dialect, this dessert is referred to as* Othmalli *or* Osmalli, *replacing the "th" sound with an "s".*

My adaptation of the recipe can be made into one large serving to be cut and shared, or made in cupcake moulds or mini tart trays for individual portions. Candy floss (the Lebanese type that is closer to dragon's beard candy than spun cotton candy) can be a special topping too. The ingredients, including the dough, can be prepared ahead of time until needed and assembled just before serving.

Separate the strings of the dough, spraying it with some water to make a little softer if it's tough, and arrange it in a 23 cm (9 in) round cake pan. Place another pan or a dish on top of the dough and weigh it down with heavy weights, such as bottles of water or bags of grain. Press for at least 1 hour and up to 3 hours to make the dough more compact.

Preheat the oven to 200°C (400°F/gas 6).

Melt the butter or ghee and pour it all over the dough until it's well covered. Bake for 15–20 minutes until golden (keep a close eye on it to avoid burning).

Remove from the oven, drain off the excess butter/ghee (reserve this to use for other recipes) and drizzle the baked pastry with the simple syrup. Set aside to cool.

Whip the cream with the sugar and rose water until you get stiff peaks.

Once the dough is cool, place on a plate and spoon dollops of the *ashta* and whipped cream over it in a random arrangement. Scatter teaspoons of the jam all over the top and sprinkle with the crushed pistachios, then serve.

SERVES 8

200 g (7 oz) kataifi dough

250 g (9 oz) butter or ghee

100 ml (generous ⅓ cup) regular simple syrup (page 103)

250 ml (1 cup) whipping cream

2 tablespoons white granulated sugar

1 tablespoon rose water

400 g (14 oz) *Ashta* (page 102)

100 g (⅓ cup) rose jam (or a jam of your preference – I also like apricot jam, berry jams or even marmalade)

30 g (¼ cup) pistachios, crushed

Baklawa Asabea'

Baklava fingers

Baklawa *is an umbrella term – so many types of sweet treats go under it. Most of them, if not all, feature a form of dough with one type, or a mixture, of nuts as a filling. In this chapter, I have chosen to feature a few types that are less common – ones that you might not find on every Middle Eastern, Levantine, Turkish or Greek restaurant menu.*

For a beginner, this is a perfect baklava to start with. Asabea' means "fingers". Typically, in sweet factories the filo (phyllo) pastry sheets used can be huge and rolling them by hand can be as tedious as rolling a large carpet. They fill part of the sheet with the nut mixture, then roll the sheet onto a thin metal rod, which makes rolling it straight much easier and faster. The sides are squeezed in along the rod, which crimps the whole roll into a thousand crinkles. The rod is then removed and the roll placed in the baking tray. This baklava is not usually baked but fried in ghee, then drowned in aromatic syrup for sweetness, but I bake it in the oven for ease.

Preheat the oven to 200°C (400°F/gas 6).

In a food processor, or in a sealable bag with a rolling pin, crush the nuts, sugar and rose water to a very fine rubble.

Take out the filo pastry sheets and lay them on the work surface. Cover them with a damp cloth while you work. Take one sheet of filo and fold the side closest to you in by a third. Spoon a sixth of the nut mix onto the pastry, arranging it along the folded edge. Roll the pastry into a sausage to cover the filling, folding in the sides as you go to hold the filling in place and keep rolling gently until the whole sheet is used. (If using larger sheets, cut them to appropriate sizes before rolling – you don't want a large thickness of pastry.) It can help to insert a thin skewer on the first fold to assist with the rolling, then take it out.

Gently move the roll to a lipped baking sheet that fits the roll snugly. Squish the roll a bit from the sides inwards to create a crinkled wave in the pastry – this creates a better crunch. Continue to fill the rest of the rolls.

Cut the outer edges of each roll with a sharp knife (I leave them in the tray to bake, they make a great cook's treat), then cut each roll into 8 pieces (or fewer, depending on your preference). Spoon over the melted butter or ghee to cover the rolls.

Bake for 20–25 minutes until slightly browned.

Take out of the oven and generously drizzle with the syrup (or honey) and leave to cool completely. They can be stored in an airtight container for 2–3 weeks.

MAKES UP TO 48 PIECES

300 g (10½ oz) pistachios (or a mix of cashews/almonds/walnuts)

4 tablespoons icing (confectioners') sugar

60 ml (¼ cup) rose water

200 g (7 oz) filo (phyllo) pastry sheets (mine come in a 23 cm/9 in square stack and I use about 6 sheets)

100 g (3½ oz) butter or ghee, melted

80–125 ml (⅓–½ cup) regular simple syrup (page 103) (or runny honey), either cold or at room temperature

Baklawa Taj el Malek

King's crown baklava

A baklava fit for a king. Literally named "the king's crown", this sweet treat is bejewelled with the best nuts, usually pistachios, carefully placed inside a coronet of kataifi vermicelli. It also sometimes called ish el belbol or bulbul, which translates to "nest of the bulbul" (a family of songbirds), because it looks rather like a nest with the precious eggs inside it.

Just like any baklava, it is covered in ghee and baked in the oven, then excess ghee is drained off after baking.

Divide the dough into separate long thin strands. Spray with water to hydrate it, if needed, to make it pliable. With a strand about 2.5 cm (1 in) wide laid on the work surface, wind the end around your thumb (or a small shot glass) and start rolling while twisting the pastry around your thumb 3 times to form a roll of pastry. Cut away the rest of the strand and tuck the loose ends under the roll. Stand the roll in a deep 23 cm (9 in) baking tray and repeat the process until all the dough is used up. You should get about 24 rolls out of the pastry.

Press the pistachios into the hollow of each dough roll, heaping them a little over the top to make a small mound. Cover with cling film (plastic wrap), then press with another tray or plate, adding a weight on top. Let sit for 1 hour, then remove the weight, cover and leave to rest for 1–2 hours.

Preheat the oven to 180°C (350°F/gas 4).

Remove the cling film and pour the melted ghee or clarified butter over the whole tray (don't worry if it's too much, it will be drained off later). Bake for 25–30 minutes until browned. (If the tops still need more browning, it can be finished under a hot grill/broiler.) Remove from the oven and drain off all the ghee.

Meanwhile, prepare the syrup by stirring the sugar and water together in a saucepan over a high heat until the sugar melts. Reduce the heat to medium and keep boiling until the mixture is clear. Add the lemon juice, remove from the heat, then add the rose water and orange blossom water.

Spoon, drizzle or brush the warm syrup over the baklava pieces, depending on how sweet you'd like them to be. Drain any excess syrup and let the pieces cool completely before storing in an airtight container for up to 1 month.

MAKES 24 PIECES

250 g (9 oz) kataifi dough (if using frozen dough, defrost completely, then bring to room temperature)

250 g (9 oz) pistachios

250 g (9 oz) ghee or clarified butter, melted

FOR THE SYRUP

165 g (¾ cup) white granulated sugar

60 ml (¼ cup) water

1 teaspoon lemon juice

1 tablespoon rose water

1 tablespoon orange blossom water

Shaabiyat

Baked filo triangles with *ashta* and pistachios

Shaabiyat is a crispy pastry parcel filled with ashta, or sometimes walnuts. The recipe has its origins in Areeha, a city in Idlib, northwest Syria. It is said that only two families used to make it there and it is thought to have existed there for the past two hundred years. It is also known as warbat, which is a reference to the diagonally folded shape. The dough is handmade with nothing but flour, salt and water and is then rolled thin with local ghee, stacked into layers and rolled again. It is then filled with ashta before baking and served doused with syrup or honey. Ready-made filo (phyllo) sheets are ideal as a shortcut. It is common to eat one on-the-go, wrapped in paper, or to take to a special lunch or dinner to be enjoyed with coffee.

Remove the filo pastry from the refrigerator to soften the dough a little. Preheat the oven to 200°C (400°F/gas 6).

Take a pile of 4–5 pastry sheets and cut them into equal squares, around 12 cm (4¾ in) each. Scoop 1–1½ tablespoons (around 40 g/1½ oz) of the *ashta* onto each square and fold the corners of each bundle of sheets diagonally to form a triangle and enclose the filling.

Arrange on a greased or lined baking tray. Repeat with the remaining dough and *ashta*.

Generously brush the triangles with melted butter or ghee, making sure not to leave any dry spots. Bake for around 20 minutes until golden.

Remove from the oven, drizzle a spoonful of simple syrup on each triangle and sprinkle a little ground pistachio in the middle of each triangle. If using, add one or two drizzles of orange blossom petal jam and let cool.

Once cooled, serve immediately or store in an airtight container and ideally eat on the day they are made.

MAKES ABOUT 12 PIECES

250 g (9 oz) filo (phyllo) pastry sheets (thawed if frozen)

500 g (1 lb 2 oz) *Ashta* (page 102), quick or luxurious process

50 g (1¾ oz) melted butter or ghee (or more, if needed)

200 ml (generous ¾ cup) simple syrup (page 103) (or more, if needed)

20 g (¾ oz) ground pistachios

orange blossom petal jam (optional)

Baklawa Ballouriye

Crystal baklava with pistachios

Ballouriye *means "crystal", so-called for the clear colour this type of baklava is supposed to have. The vermicelli or kataifi pastry is not supposed to brown but just dry out, and the white colour contrasts beautifully with green of the pistachios. It is a striking dessert to make and share. The syrup added at the end brings all the ingredients together and binds them, which makes it easier to cut into serving portions.*

Make sure you have two 23 cm (9 in) baking trays that can fit into one another. Grease one of the trays with half the butter or ghee.

Lightly spray the kataifi with water to hydrate it, then pull the strands apart to separate them. Arrange half of the pastry in the base of the greased baking tray, making sure to allow some to run along the sides a little. Cover with cling film (plastic wrap) or baking paper. Place the second baking tray on top and weigh it down with a heavy water bottle or weights. Press for at least 1 hour. (Keep the other half of the kataifi covered in the meantime.)

Lightly toast the pistachios in a dry pan until just fragrant. Set aside to cool.

Once cooled, mix the pistachios with the light syrup. Remove the cling film from the pressed kataifi and spread the nut mixture over the top. Cover with a layer of the remaining kataifi. Cover again with cling film, return the baking tray and weights, and press for at least 2 hours.

Once ready to bake, preheat the oven to 150°C (300°F/gas 2).

Remove the cling film and bake the *ballouriye* for 5–10 minutes, making sure it doesn't take on any colour. Remove from the oven and shake a little to release it from the tray. Grease the second tray with the remaining butter/ghee, then flip the *ballouriye* into that tray. Return to the oven and bake for 5–10 minutes, again making sure it doesn't take on any colour. Remove from the oven.

Cover the empty tray with a layer of cling film. Place the cooked baklava in it, then cover it with the thick syrup. Cover the top of the baklava with cling film, top with the other tray and the weights and leave for a further 2 hours to press it into shape.

Use a sharp, serrated knife to cut into pieces and serve. If generously covered with sugar syrup it will keep in an airtight container for to 2–4 weeks.

Pictured overleaf

MAKES ABOUT 30 PIECES

50 g (1¾ oz) butter or ghee, melted

300 g (10½ oz) kataifi dough

400 g (14 oz) pistachios

100 ml (generous ⅓ cup) light simple syrup (page 103)

500 ml (2 cups) thick simple syrup (page 103)

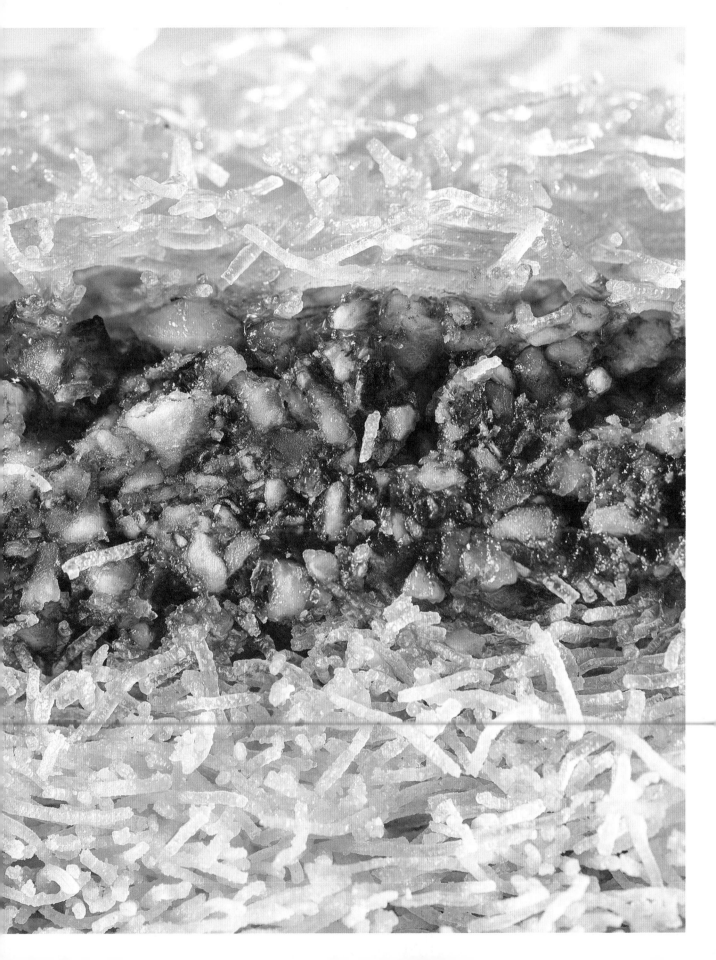

Baklawa Borma

Rolled baklava

Borma, *or* mabroumé *as it is called in some areas of Syria, refers to the round or rolled shape of this baklava. Considered to be the most sugary type of baklava, for this version I found a balance that allows the rolls to hold their shape but not be not so sweet that you couldn't eat an entire batch (we almost did) before getting a sugar rush. It is made with a type of kataifi that – according to my favourite sweet shop in Beirut, Al Rachidi – is different to the type used for* Osmalliye *(page 104) or* Knefe *(page 121). I couldn't tell the difference, so I urge you to use whatever type you can get your hands on. It takes some skill to perfect this type of baklava, but it is not impossible. It took me two or three messy attempts before I began to make ones I could show off and give others to try. Don't despair – keep practising.*

Place the nuts in a food processor and crush until slightly broken, or chop into rough quarters with a knife, or place them in a sealable bag and smack them with a heavy object until crushed. Mix with the light simple syrup (or honey) and set aside.

Divide the kataifi into 3 equal portions by weight (in my case, it gave me 3 full strands and a small one that I pulled apart to distribute equally). Wrap them in a damp dish towel as the strands need to remain pliable. Take one of the portions, rub it between your palm to loosen the individual strands and lay on a flat surface. Place a third of the nut mixture along the middle of the long bundle of strands. Tuck the end nearest you over (as though you're tucking the bottom of a wrap) and start rolling the strands over the filling at a diagonal angle – somewhere between 45° and 90°. Keep holding the first part and roll it with one hand, use your other hand to help keep the nuts in place while you roll. Once all of it is rolled, tuck the ends of the pastry in and tighten the roll with an action as if you were wringing a wet cloth. Place on a rectangular oven tray that snugly fits the length of the roll.

Repeat with the remaining dough and filling to make 2 more rolls.

Cover the surface of the rolls with cling film (plastic wrap), then place another oven tray of the same size (or a wooden board or any flat surface that fits) over the rolls and weigh down with a heavy object. Leave to press for at least 1–2 hours or overnight.

MAKES ABOUT 30 PIECES

300 g (10½ oz) nuts of choice
  (pine nuts, cashews or pistachios)
60 ml (¼ cup) light simple syrup
  (page 103) (or honey)
400 g (14 oz) kataifi dough
400 g (14 oz) ghee or clarified butter
1 × quantity regular simple syrup
  (page 103), hot

When ready to bake, preheat the oven to 200°C (400°F/gas 6) and melt your ghee or clarified butter.

Pour the melted ghee over the rolls, making sure to coat them well with the whole amount. Bake for 30 minutes.

At this point, flip the rolls over with tongs or a spatula, return to the oven and bake for another 30 minutes, making sure they don't burn. They need to be a deep golden brown colour and crisp all the way through.

Meanwhile, prepare your regular simple syrup, ensuring it is hot.

Once the rolls are fully baked, tilt the tray to drain off all the ghee. Drench the rolls generously in the simple syrup while both are still hot. Allow the rolls to cool in the syrup for 10 minutes, then remove to a wire rack set over a tray to allow the excess syrup to drain. Leave to cool completely, at least 3 hours.

When cool, diagonally cut across the rolls with a serrated knife in a sawing motion into 2–3 cm (1 in) pieces. You should get about 10 pieces from each roll. (The doughy offcuts at the ends can be crushed in a food processor and used on top of fruits, *ashta*, granola bowls, or as the base of a cheesecake.)

Store in an airtight container for up to 2 months. The sugar and fat should have removed all moisture from the baklava, so it should keep for that long, but discard if any mould starts to develop.

Mwara'a

Lazy walnut and almond baklava

MAKES ABOUT 12 PIECES

FOR THE DOUGH

175 g (scant 1¼ cups) plain (all-purpose) flour

100 ml (generous ⅓ cup) water

½ teaspoon dried active yeast

¼ teaspoon salt

1 teaspoon white granulated sugar

1 tablespoon olive oil, plus extra for greasing the bowl

FOR THE FILLING

75 g (2¾ oz) almonds

75 g (2¾ oz) walnuts

2 tablespoons icing (confectioners') sugar

1 teaspoon rose water

TO FINISH

4 tablespoons butter or ghee, melted

icing (confectioners') sugar, for dusting, or honey for drizzling

There is a popular bakery in Amchit, a coastal town close to Byblos in the northern part of Lebanon, called Furn Al Sabaya (The Ladies' Bakery) and it is run by three or four women. They specialise in qors beid (manouche with awarma and an egg in its centre) as well as this recipe. Mwara'a loosely translates to "layered". The dough is rolled thin and a nut filling is placed in the centre. A small hole is poked in the middle, then the dough is rolled outwards around the filling until a large circular rope is achieved (see overleaf). This is then brought together in a rough coil shape, baked and dusted with powdered sugar. The rolling technique is an acquired skill and requires a very well-rolled and relaxed dough to prevent the dough from retracting in on itself. For this easier version, I roll the dough into a rectangle and roll it around the filling like a cinnamon roll before coiling it.

Mix all the ingredients for the dough and knead until the dough comes together. Return to the bowl with a little oil, cover and leave to rest for at least 1 hour.

Pulse the filling ingredients in a food processor until roughly chopped.

Use a rolling pin to roll out the dough into a rectangle, as wide and as thin as you can. Brush with half of the butter or ghee and sprinkle with the filling. Roll the dough up from a long edge into a log, then coil up like a snail. Transfer to a baking sheet, cover and leave to rest for 10 minutes.

Preheat the oven to 200°C (400°F/gas 6).

Brush the dough with the butter or ghee for finishing and bake for 15 minutes until golden. Immediately dust with icing sugar or drizzle with honey. Cut into pieces and serve.

Knefe/Knafe Nabulsiye

Baked kataifi with sweet cheese

This traybake of semolina or kataifi pastry with cheese is baked and drizzled with simple syrup and served warm. The most common form of knefe *(spelled the Lebanese way) is made with semolina dough (*farek *or* fark al knefeh*) and is served in a sesame bun (ka'ak) that is stuffed until it is overflowing with the* knefe *right from the hot tray. The dough can be approximated with ground-up kataifi pastry in the absence of the real thing. The Lebanese eat* knefe *for breakfast and it was common when I was younger and partying to the early hours of the morning to have* knefe *on the way back home.*

The other form is knafe Nabulsiye *(spelled the Palestinian or Jordanian way). It is the same, but made with kataifi and commonly served on a plate. You have the choice of na'emi (soft), which has ground-up kataifi as a base, or kheshne (coarse), which is made with the long strands visible on top of the cheese. The dough in* knafe Nabulsiye *is dyed orange, which contrasts with the ground pistachios sprinkled on top of each serving.*

SERVES 6

100 g (3½ oz) butter, melted, plus extra for greasing
250 g (9 oz) kataifi pastry
5 saffron strands (or orange food colouring) for *knafe Nabulsiye* (optional)
orange food colouring for *knafe Nabulsiye* (optional)
500 g (generous 3 cups) grated cheese (I use desalinated Czech Akkawi, mozzarella or queso fresco)
small sesame-seeded buns (ka'ak), to serve (optional)
ground pistachios, to serve (optional, if making *knafe Nabulsiye*)

FOR THE SYRUP

125 ml (½ cup) water
230 g (1 cup) caster (superfine) sugar
1 tablespoon lemon juice
1 tablespoon orange blossom water
1½ teaspoons rose water

Make the syrup first so that it has time to cool. Combine the water and sugar in a saucepan and bring to the boil. Cook until the sugar has dissolved completely and the mixture bubbles and becomes clear. Remove from the heat and add the lemon juice and aromatic waters. Allow to cool completely.

Preheat the oven to 200°C (400°F/gas 6). Grease the bottom and sides of a shallow 30 cm (12 in) round cake pan with butter.

For Lebanese *knefe*, blend the butter with the kataifi pastry in a food processor until it looks like wet sand.

For *knafe Nabulsiye*, pour 60 ml (¼ cup) of boiling water over the saffron and cool completely before mixing into the butter. This will give a yellow colour to the pastry. For the orange colour seen in pastry shops, mix a drop of orange food colouring into the butter. Place the pastry in a bowl, pour over the butter and gently massage until covered without breaking up the pastry too much.

Press the pastry into the prepared cake pan, covering the base and sides, and top with the grated cheese. Bake for around 20 minutes until the cheese has melted completely.

Remove from the oven and flip the *knefe* out onto a serving tray or plate. Douse with the cooled syrup. Cut into portions and serve immediately, either plated or in a small sesame bun. If making *knafe Nabulsiye*, sprinkle the top with ground pistachios before serving.

Store in an airtight container and refrigerate for up to 5 days or freeze for a month. Can be reheated in the oven or microwave to serve.

Halawet el Shmayse

Rice sweets with *ashta* from Tripoli

On the large steps at the end of the Tripoli souk lies a small shop that you could easily miss. Even if you find the shop, you might find it closed if it's lunch or prayer time. But persevere, as you must taste the unique sweets they make. The shop is now owned by Nouh Al Haddad, who inherited it from his father, indeed the lineage goes back at least five generations (their photos are framed and hung behind the counter). Their halawet el shmayse is exceptional. A Greek chef and restaurateur I took there once called it the Lebanese mochi for its soft, sweet and stretchy texture and creamy filling. I suggest trying it in Tripoli, if possible, but making it at home is the second-best option.

Soak the rice in the measured water for at least 2 hours, or ideally overnight.

When ready to prepare, place the rice and its soaking water in a large saucepan and bring to the boil, then reduce the heat to low and cook, stirring occasionally, until the water is absorbed but before the rice starts sticking to the bottom of the pan. The rice should be mushy. Remove from the heat and use a stick blender to purée the rice until smooth.

Pound the mastic with a tablespoon of the sugar to help it break down. Add it to the rice purée with the rest of the sugar.

Place back over a low heat and stir the mixture until most of the water evaporates – you will notice that it will thicken even more. It is ready when a spoon dragged across the bottom of the pan leaves a clear streak and takes a second to be covered. This will usually take up to 50 minutes. Once thickened, let the mixture cool.

Pour a third of the icing sugar into a 20 cm (8 in) square container that is about 5 cm (2 in) deep and spread to cover the base. Place the rice mixture into the container and cover with another third of the icing sugar. Chill in the refrigerator overnight.

To assemble, take a piece of the rice mixture the size of a ping pong ball and flatten it into a thin disc with a rolling pin on a work surface dusted in the remaining icing sugar. Place a tablespoon of *ashta* on top. You can pinch in the sides to enclose the filling and shape into balls that resemble mochi, or fold over into pockets or rolls. Decorate with ground pistachios, if desired.

MAKES ABOUT 30

125 g (generous ½ cup) short-grain rice

500 ml (2 cups) water

2 small pieces of mastic

250 g (generous 1 cup) white granulated sugar

150 g (1¼ cups) icing (confectioners') sugar (or more as needed)

400 g (14 oz) *Ashta* (page 102), long process

30 g (1 oz) ground pistachios (optional)

Halawet el Jeben

Sweet cheese and semolina rolls with *ashta*

It's not quite clear where this recipe originates – it has been attributed to Hama, a city in west-central Syria not too far from North Lebanon, and also to the nearby city of Homs. Regardless, its popularity has reached far and wide, even to Berlin in Germany, where a large Syrian community can be found. It is common to find this in most sweet shops in Lebanon, but it is the shops around Tripoli that make it best.

Made from a dough of semolina and Akkawi cheese that is filled with ashta and drizzled with a fragrant syrup of rose water and orange blossom water, I call these sweet cheese rolls. Usually you see them sold as small, filled, two-bite rolls, but in Tripoli you can find a version where the dough is shredded by hand, or cut into fettuccine-like strips, then served topped with the ashta and syrup. Both are delicious.

If using Akkawi cheese, shred it and rinse it two or three times in clean water until it is no longer salty. Drain well.

Combine the water and sugar in a large saucepan, set it over a medium heat, cook until the sugar is dissolved. Add the semolina and mix until the liquid has been absorbed and the mixture looks like wet sand. Add three-quarters of the cheese and mix well with a wooden spoon or sturdy spatula until most of the cheese has melted and the mixture starts to thicken. Add the rest of the cheese and mix until it's all incorporated. Keep mixing until the mixture dries out a little more and the cheese is completely emulsified, resulting in a continuous cheese pull when the mix is lifted with the spoon. Remove from the heat and leave to cool slightly until it's warm enough to touch.

Brush your work surface with a little simple syrup, transfer the dough to it and knead until the dough is firm. From here you have a choice: the home-style option or pastry chef's style.

For the home-style option, cut the warm dough into 4 pieces and roll each piece out, adding more syrup if needed to prevent it from sticking (or roll out between 2 sheets of cling film/plastic wrap), to a rectangle about 2–3 mm (⅛ in) thick. Set the pieces aside to dry out.

MAKES 25

450 g (1 lb) Czech Akkawi cheese (or mozzarella)
250 ml (1 cup) water
50 g (scant ¼ cup) white granulated sugar
250 g (2 cups) fine semolina
250 ml (1 cup) light simple syrup (page 103), plus extra to serve
500 g (1 lb 2 oz) *Ashta* (page 102)

TO GARNISH

50 g (1¾ oz) pistachios, crushed
orange blossom petal jam

For the pastry chef's style, roll out the warm dough ball to a large circle, adding more simple syrup as needed. Brush the base of a 40–50 cm (16–20 in) circular baking tray with more syrup and place the dough on it. Raise the tray on a small stool or anything that can prop up the tray away from the surface underneath it. Start stretching each side of the dough over the edge of the tray and let gravity and the pastry's own weight help pull it down and stretch it out. The dough must be still be warm for it to stretch. Stretch it as much as you can, then leave it to cool and dry out before transferring it back to the work surface.

Cut either style of dough into 10 cm (4 in) squares and fill each one with 1 teaspoon of *ashta*. Fold in the edges and roll up to enclose the filling. Arrange on a serving plate or tray and garnish each roll with a little crushed pistachio and some orange blossom petal jam.

Refrigerate until ready to serve. Serve with extra syrup, if desired.

Offcuts of the dough can be pressed into a ring mould and simply topped with *ashta* and the garnishes, or cut into strips and served like fettuccine with the *ashta* and garnishes on top.

Alternatively, the dough can be stored in the refrigerator and the sweets assembled just before serving.

Mafrouke/Daoukiye

Layered pistachio pastry with *ashta*

Mafrouke is a simple dessert made with farek or fark al knefeh (a processed semolina dough where the semolina is first roasted and ground to a fine crumb, then mixed with ghee and aromatic syrup to make a soft dough) topped a layer of ashta cream. Daoukiye is a similar recipe but is made with pistachios, which gives the dough a green colour, and the cream is sandwiched between two layers of dough. Sweet shops sometimes enhance the hue with green food colouring, which you can do too, if you like. It is named for a shop in Al Dahye, the southern suburb of Beirut, run by the Al Daouk family who are the most well known for making it in Beirut, especially during Ramadan. Other sweet shops started making it too, but they call it mafrouket festo' *(pistachio mafrouke). I have taken a few shortcuts in this recipe to make it easier to make at home.*

Break apart the kataifi dough, or pulse it in a food processor to fine grounds. Toss in a frying pan with the butter and toast over a medium-low heat until toasted and crispy. Set aside to cool.

Pulse the pistachios in the food processor until finely ground. Add the cooled kataifi and pulse until combined. Add the icing sugar and syrup and blend until combined. If you like, you can add the rose water here to make it more fragrant. If the paste is too thick, add a little water to thin it. The texture should resemble a unbaked pie crust, but slightly stickier. Cover and let it sit for 30 minutes.

To assemble, press half the dough into a ring mould on a plate. Top with the *ashta*. (For a neat finish, you can also use a piping bag to pipe 6–8 circles of the *ashta* to designate individual portions.) Press the other half of the dough on the work surface between 2 sheets of baking paper or cling film (plastic wrap). Cut out a disc the same size as the ring mould and place on top of the *ashta* layer. Decorate with ground pistachios and rose petals or orange blossom jam.

Serve with extra syrup on the side, if you wish.

SERVES 6–8

140 g (5 oz) kataifi dough

40 g (1½ oz) butter

200 g (7 oz) pistachios

50 g (scant ½ cup) icing (confectioners') sugar

60 ml (¼ cup) light simple syrup (page 103), plus extra to serve (optional)

1 tablespoon rose water (optional)

500 g (1 lb 2 oz) *Ashta* (page 102)

TO DECORATE

30 g (3–4 tablespoons) ground pistachios

rose petals or orange blossom jam

NOTE

You can also assemble the *mafrouke* in a casserole dish using the same process and cut it with a knife to serve. Alternatively, you can flatten the dough into individual pieces, fill with *ashta*, then seal for individual portions.

Cookies
& Cakes

Most Lebanese cookies are associated with celebrations and they have a rather long shelf life. They tend to be quite small and time-consuming to make – not because they are difficult to prepare, but rather that they are made in large volumes, enough to serve guests and give away to friends. As a result, it has become a habit to gather in groups at the homes of friends and relations to help make their cookies when they are needed.

These gatherings might happen for big celebrations, for instance to make *Maamoul* (page 132) for all the major holidays, or as entertainment on a winter's night, when we might make *Malateet* (page 141) and make use of the traditional metal heater that comes with an oven. They are perfect times to catch up, talk and gossip with friends, or find an excuse to meet up with a crush in a setting that doesn't seem suspicious or untoward!

Whenever we made cookies, my mom and grandma used to tell us not to count them as it would remove or reduce the blessings in them. I'm not sure where that belief comes from but I still believe that there is a blessing in making

and sharing homemade food. We still practice the courtesy of never returning a container empty whenever someone brings us food from their own home. We will make cookies or a cake and send a few pieces back in the container when we return it. This might be a dying practice now, but I hold true to it.

There aren't many traditional cakes (in the conventional sense) in Lebanese cuisine. Most common are sheet-pan cakes with simple ingredients, rather than elaborate layer cakes. But we do get inspired by recipes we try and love from other countries (popular when I was growing up in the 1990s was the *Forêt Noire* or Black Forest gâteau (page 155), which seemed to feature at every birthday party along with the jello cups and custard). I still love to make cakes for birthdays and other celebrations for nostalgia's sake.

I have included a few traditional Lebanese favourites in this chapter, such as *Sfouf* (page 153) and *Sfouf bi Debes* (page 154); and a Palestinian delicacy, *Qizha* (page 156), along with some inventions of my own, including an indulgent twist on a Basque cheesecake with the flavours of baklava (page 158).

Maamoul

Filled butter cookies for Easter or Eid

The one cookie that everyone in Arab countries makes and somehow agrees on is maamoul. *These semolina butter cookies are filled with dates, walnuts or pistachios and are made on major holidays. For Christians, they are made for Easter, while Muslims make them for Al Adha and Al Fitr. Commercial* mammoul *are shape-coded to distinguish the different fillings.*

Making maamoul *has always been a gathering and a tradition. When I lived with my family in the refugee camp, with the houses so close to each other, I could pick up the aromas of butter, orange blossom, rose water and frankincense on every local walk in the days preceding Easter, when people would bake the cookies at home or the local bakeries would be busy preparing them for the celebration. Except on Saturdays – that day was reserved for making Ka'ak Asfar (page 31).*

I grew up with my mom making maamoul *with my her mother-in-law, Teta Halloun, or with my grandma's friend, our neighbour Zakiye. The shapes would be made by pressing the cookies into a greased wooden mould, which is then smacked hard on the work surface to release them – a symphony of percussion beats if ever you heard it. Sometimes the mould could be slipped into a clean nylon stocking to release the cookies faster. Eventually, Zakiye encouraged my mom to ditch the mould and joined our gathering to help shape the* maamoul *manually, pinching them with a special tweezer to create a unique pattern on each cookie. Zakiye passed away in 2022. I am grateful to her for helping us learn to make* maamoul *this way and we remember her each time we make them.*

*MAKES 30–40
(ENOUGH FOR 1 PORTION OF DATE FILLING OR FOR THE PISTACHIO AND WALNUT FILLINGS COMBINED)*

225 g (8 oz) butter, softened
1½ tablespoons white granulated sugar
2 teaspoons ground mahlab
375 g (3 cups) fine semolina
125 g (1 cup) coarse semolina
60 ml (¼ cup) rose water
60 ml (¼ cup) orange blossom water
¼ teaspoon instant dried yeast
1 piece of charcoal
1 small piece of natural rose incense
150 g (1¼ cups) icing (confectioners') sugar (optional)

method and fillings continue overleaf

In a large bowl, rub the butter, sugar, mahlab and both types of semolina together with half of the rose and orange blossom waters between both hands until the mixture resembles wet sand. Cover and set aside overnight, or for at least 10 hours.

The next day, add the yeast and the rest of the flower waters and knead with your hands until it forms a dough. Kneading is an important step here, as it ensures the cookies won't crack when baking.

Light the charcoal and put it in an incense burner or on a small plate, then place the piece of rose incense on top. With the dough still in its mixing bowl, make a hole or dimple in the dough, place the plate or incense burner in the dimple and cover the bowl with a piece of cloth for around 15 minutes, or until the incense stops burning.

Preheat the oven to 200°C (400°F/gas 6).

Maamoul cont.

FOR THE DATE FILLING

500 g (1 lb 2 oz) date paste
(or pitted dates)

½ teaspoon ground nutmeg

½ teaspoon ground cloves

½ teaspoon ground cinnamon

½ teaspoon ground mahlab

10 g (¼ oz) butter, softened

FOR THE PISTACHIO FILLING

250 g (2 cups) pistachios, medium
ground

90 g (¾ cup) icing
(confectioners') sugar

1 teaspoon ground mahlab

2 tablespoons rose water
(or more to taste)

FOR THE WALNUT FILLING

250 g (2 cups) walnuts, medium
ground (or a mix of walnuts and
almonds)

90 g (¾ cup) icing (confectioners')
sugar

1 teaspoon ground mahlab

2 tablespoons rose water,
(or more to taste)

½ teaspoon ground cinnamon

Meanwhile, make your chosen filling/s. For the date filling, mix all the ingredients together and shape into balls (just smaller than a ping pong ball) and set aside, covered. To make the pistachio or walnut fillings simply mix the filling ingredients together in a bowl. They should be slightly damp and sticky.

Prepare the dough by rolling it into balls the size of ping pong balls (about 20 g/½ oz each). Keep them covered when you are not rolling them out. One at a time, flatten each ball between your palms or poke a hole into it with your index finger while rotating the ball to thin all the sides. Place a small ball or a tablespoon of filling inside and seal the ball of dough.

Typically, each filling is shaped differently. For the date-filled cookies, press the filled ball of dough to form a thick disc, then use the small round end of a wooden spoon to press the centre of the disc to about three-quarters depth until it forms a mini bagel-shaped cookie. Pistachio *maamoul* are shaped into finger cookies, while walnut *maamoul* are shaped into domes.

I like to pinch a pattern with the serrated edge of *maamoul* tongs all over to decorate the filled balls. You can also use a *maamoul* mould to shape them. My tip for turning them out without sticking is to cover the mould with a clean nylon stocking, push the filled dough ball into the mould, then bash it on the edge of the table with your hand underneath to catch the shaped *maamoul* as it falls.

Place the shaped cookies on a baking sheet and bake for 15 minutes until the tops and bottoms are lightly golden.

Dust with icing sugar, if desired, and let them cool before storing in an airtight container for up to 1 month.

Karabeej Maa Natef

Pistachio butter cookies with meringue

MAKES ABOUT 30

FOR THE KARABEEJ DOUGH

200 g (generous 1½ cups) fine semolina

100 g (⅔ cup) plain (all-purpose) flour

1 tablespoon caster (superfine) sugar

¼ teaspoon instant dried yeast

150 g (5½ oz) butter

1 teaspoon ground mahlab

2 tablespoons rose water

2 tablespoons orange blossom water

FOR THE FILLING

100 g (3½ oz) shelled pistachios, plus
    extra to serve

60 g (½ cup) icing
    (confectioners') sugar

½ teaspoon ground mahlab

1 tablespoon melted butter

1 tablespoon rose water

FOR THE MERINGUE (EGG WHITE OR SOAPWORT NATEF)

75 ml (⅓ cup) soapwort root water
    (see below)
    OR
100 g (3½ oz) egg whites
    (from 3 eggs)
    1 tablespoon lemon juice
170 g (¾ cup) caster (superfine) sugar
60 ml (¼ cup) water

FOR THE SOAPWORT ROOT WATER

50 g (1¾ oz) soapwort root (buy online
    or in health food stores)

600 ml (20½ fl oz) water

Method continues overleaf

There used to be a man who would stand outside the church at 11 am on Sundays after mass with a bucket of meringue and pistachio butter cookies, and some dice. Children could buy the number of cookies they liked or they could throw the dice and receive as many cookies as the number they threw. My mom never let me get any because she was worried that the natef meringue was made with egg whites and would have spoiled on his long trip to sell the cookies. But while researching for this book I looked up an ingredient I had heard about many times: Saponaria officinalis or soapwort. In Arabic, it is known as halawe (halva) root, since the extract from the root is used as an important agent in making halawe (page 200). In this recipe, the root extract is whipped instead of egg whites and stabilised with a hot sugar syrup and vanilla if desired. The outcome is a light fluffy meringue that is shelf and temperature stable. It finally became clear why the karabeej seller could sell his products for so long.

I should note that soapwort extract should always be used in moderation – large amounts can have negative side effects (the root extract is also used to wash wool or carpets!). For ease, I have also offered a traditional egg white meringue here.

Put the semolina, flour, sugar and yeast in a large bowl, then rub in the butter. Add the mahlab and aromatic waters, mix well, then knead well until the dough is soft and elastic. Cover with a damp cloth and set aside for at least 2 hours.

For the filling, pulse the pistachios in a food processor until coarsely ground. Add the icing sugar, mahlab, butter and rose water and pulse until combined.

Knead the rested dough a few times until pliable. If the dough is too warm and loose, refrigerate it for 15 minutes.

Preheat the oven to 200°C (400°F/Gas 6).

Take a quarter of the dough and roll it out into a long thin rectangle about 4 mm (¼ in) thick. Take a quarter of the filling and lay it down the middle of the rectangle, then roll in the sides to enclose it. Give the log a roll back and forth on the work surface to seal it and cut with a sharp knife into little fingers, around 5 cm (2 in) long. Place on a lined baking sheet and prick with a fork all over. Repeat until all the dough and filling is used up.

Bake for 12–14 minutes until lightly golden. Cool completely before transferring to a sealed container.

For the meringue: if making the *natef* with soapwort root, wash the root well, then soak it in the measured water for 12 hours. Place the mixture in a saucepan, bring to a simmer and cook until reduced by two-thirds. Strain into a jar and refrigerate. This will make more than you need, but it can be refrigerated for up to a week.

In a large bowl or a stand mixer fitted with a whisk, whisk the measured soapwort water for around 5 minutes until frothy and fluffy like beaten egg whites.

If making egg white meringue, beat the egg whites and lemon juice in a large bowl with an electric beater to stiff peaks.

In a small saucepan, combine the sugar and water and gently stir over a medium heat until combined. Bring to the boil and cook, stirring, for around 10 minutes, or until the syrup reaches 115°C (240°F).

Pour the syrup in a thin stream over the whipped egg whites (or soapwort root water) while beating continuously until the whole amount is incorporated and the mixture turns glossy. Transfer to a container and leave to cool completely.

To serve, add a big dollop of the meringue to the middle of a plate, or into a bowl placed on a plate, and arrange the cookies around it. Decorate with extra ground pistachios.

The meringue *natef* will keep for up to 2 days in an airtight container in the refrigerator, whereas soapwort *natef* will keep for up to a week. The cookies will last for 1–2 weeks in an airtight container.

Malateet

Palestinian vegan anise cookies

Lent is the month of fasting observed by Christians before Easter. Traditionally, Christians would abstain from consuming all forms of animal products, including dairy and eggs, for the whole period of Lent. We didn't abstain from having sweets though, unless someone had personally vowed to give them up. Therefore the recipe repertoire included a lot of vegan sweets that could also be made with simple ingredients found at home. Malateet is a recipe I know only Christian Palestinians make. Similar anise-flavoured cookies do exist, but this combination of ingredients and dotted shape are unique to this type of cookie. The shape is reminiscent of Maakroun (pages 174–5), except these are baked rather than fried and are definitely less sweet.

Preheat the oven to 200°C (400°F/gas 6). Line several baking sheets with baking paper.

Mix the flour, oil, sugar, sesame seeds, mahlab and baking powder in a large bowl.

If using ground aniseed: mix it in, then add most of the water and bring the dough together by hand, adding more water as needed, until a firm dough comes together.

If using whole aniseeds: bring the water to the boil in a saucepan, add the seeds and boil for 5 minutes. Strain out the seeds, reserving the water and add it to the dough as above.

Take balls of dough, each roughly the size of a ping pong ball, and shape into rough long oval shapes. Place the ovals on the largest side of a box grater (or a colander) and, pushing gently with 3 fingers, slide down the holes until the exterior surface curls and becomes textured. Arrange the cookies on the baking sheets, leaving a small distance between them.

Bake for around 12 minutes, or until golden.

Cool and store in an airtight container, where they can last for up to a couple of months.

MAKES ABOUT 30

450 g (3 cups) plain (all-purpose) flour
125 ml (½ cup) olive oil (or half olive oil and half vegetable oil)
110 g (½ cup) white granulated sugar
1 tablespoon sesame seeds
1 teaspoon ground mahlab
½ teaspoon baking powder
1½ teaspoons ground aniseed (or 2 tablespoons whole aniseeds)
125 ml (½ cup) water, or as needed

Ghraybe

Crumbly butter cookies

The texture of this cookie is one I have always loved. It is crumbly and melts in your mouth with a sweet buttery mouthfeel. Well, it is made with little more than sugar, butter and flour. The iconic look of ghraybe is a pale cookie that has been baked until just set but has not taken on any colour. Simply decorated with a pistachio sliver, they are an elegant treat.

Preheat the oven to 150°C (300°F/gas 2).

Pound the mastic with a teaspoon of the icing sugar in a pestle and mortar until well ground. Set aside.

Cream the remaining icing sugar and butter in a large bowl with an electric beater until very pale and creamy, around 5–7 minutes. Add the flour and mastic and beat to incorporate. Add the orange blossom water and knead by hand until the dough is cohesive but very slightly crumbly (you may need a little more orange blossom water if the dough is too dry). Roll into a log, wrap in cling film (plastic wrap) and refrigerate for 15 minutes. If not baking immediately, you can store it for longer, but when ready to bake, rest at room temperature until less stiff to handle.

Divide the dough into 4 pieces. Cover the rest while working with one piece. Roll into a 1 cm (½ in) rope, then cut it into 6–7 equal pieces. Roll each piece into a ball shape, then press lightly with your thumb to make an indentation. Alternatively, coil each piece into a ring shape. Place on a lined baking sheet. Top each piece with a pistachio half. Repeat with the other pieces of dough.

Bake for 12–14 minutes, making sure they don't take on any colour.

Cool completely before moving as they will be fragile. Store in an airtight container for up to 2 weeks.

MAKES ABOUT 30

5 small pieces of mastic

80 g (⅔ cup) icing (confectioners') sugar

125 g (4½ oz) butter, softened

200 g (1⅓ cups) plain (all-purpose) flour

1 teaspoon orange blossom water (or more as needed)

15–20 pistachios, soaked and split in half

Kaak al Abbas

Spiced Abbas cookies

Kaak al Abbas *is a spiced cookie recipe linked to those belonging to the Shia sect in Lebanon. These cookies are prepared for Ashoura (although they are now also available in bakeries year round), which is on the tenth day of the month of Muharram, the first month of the Hijri year. Ashoura is commemorated by Shia Muslims as a day of mourning for the death of Al Hussain, the grandson of Prophet Muhammad. At this time, a majlis (condolences gathering) is held to share stories about the battle of Karbala and remember the martyrdom of Al Hussain. A mawkab (procession) is also held in the streets with chants for the occasion and mourning practices such as beating of the chest or striking the face with their hands to remember the suffering of the martyr. In a majlis, food is prepared or brought to the tent to be delivered to people in need or shared with those present. Hreese (shreds of meat cooked with wholewheat into a porridge) is a common recipe, along with* kaak al Abbas.

MAKES 8

250 g (1⅔ cups) plain (all-purpose)
  or strong (bread) flour
125 g (1 cup) fine semolina
100 ml (generous ⅓ cup) vegetable oil
1 tablespoon sesame seeds
½ teaspoon instant dried yeast
½ teaspoon baking powder
½ teaspoon salt
½ teaspoon ground ginger
½ teaspoon ground cinnamon
¼ teaspoon ground nutmeg
1 teaspoon ground aniseed
1 teaspoon ground mahlab
200 ml (generous ¾ cup) milk, warmed
150 g (⅔ cup) caster (superfine) sugar
1 teaspoon ground turmeric
olive oil, for shaping

NOTE
If you prefer the cookies to be crunchier, skip the yeast and baking powder and press them into thinner discs.

In a glass bowl, or a bowl that won't stain, mix the flour and semolina. Add the vegetable oil and rub well until the mixture resembles wet sand. Mix in the sesame seeds, yeast, baking powder, salt, ginger, cinnamon, nutmeg, anise and mahlab. Leave to rest while you prepare the wet mixture.

Warm the milk in a saucepan and stir in the sugar and turmeric until dissolved. Let it sit for a minute, then add to the flour mixture and stir until incorporated. Knead for a minute until the dough comes together. Cover and rest for 1–2 hours (this time will depend on the ambient temperature in your kitchen) or up to 12 hours (or overnight) to let the semolina absorb the liquid and the dough rest.

Preheat the oven to 180°C (350°F/gas 4).

To make the cookies, rub your hands with a teaspoon of olive oil and scoop the dough out of the bowl. Divide into 8 equal balls and roll between your palms to coat with the olive oil from your hands. Add more olive oil, if needed.

Press each ball into a disc, 8–10 cm (3¼–4 in) in diameter. Press the lid of a plastic bottle onto the surface of the dough in concentric circles or to create any pattern you'd like. Alternatively, you can press the dough into a special mould to create a pattern, ensuring the mould is well greased. Place on a lined baking tray.

Bake for 15 minutes or until golden.

Cool completely and store in an airtight container for up to 7 days.

Barazek

Syrian pistachio and sesame cookies

Originating in Damascus, Syria, during Ottoman times, these double-sided butter cookies are a classic gift to get for people when returning from a visit to Damascus. In later years, these cookies started to be made in Lebanon and Palestine as well. Palestinians feel that Al-Qods barazek (barazek from Jerusalem) are special and have something extra that barazek from other places don't have (see also Ka'ak Al-Qods, page 38). Most of us in Lebanon have never tasted barazek from Al-Qods, unless they were smuggled out through Jordan or another country and then imported. Back in the 1980s, some were fortunate to be able to go to the occupied Palestinian territories and come back. Since the majority of us can't do this even if we carry a foreign passport, Lebanese people link barazek to Damascus and believe that nothing tops the ones from there. I brought so many boxes back with me as gifts when I went for a quick visit in 2019. It is a place I would love to explore further.

MAKES ABOUT 60

120 g (4½ oz) cold or frozen butter

250 g (1⅔ cups) plain (all-purpose) flour

50 g (scant ¼ cup) white granulated sugar

½ teaspoon fine salt

50 ml (scant ¼ cup) cold water

100 g (⅔ cup) sesame seeds

2 tablespoons regular simple syrup (page 103) (or honey)

60 g (generous ⅓ cup) pistachios

NOTE

For an authentic version, try to make the cookies as thin as possible. Press them well into the pistachios until they're as thin as you can successfully still hold together before pressing them into the toasted sesame. The thinner, the better. They will be crunchy and not soft and crumbly.

Grate the butter into a mixing bowl, then mix in the flour, kneading it with your fingers until you get a wet sand texture. (You could also pulse it a few times in a food processor.)

Stir the sugar and salt into the cold water (there isn't enough water for it to dissolve completely, but that is fine). Add the water to the dough and start mixing. The dough will break but keep kneading until it comes back together and cleans the sides of the bowl. Cover and refrigerate for 1 hour, or until ready to use.

Preheat the oven to 180°C (350°F/gas 4). Line a baking sheet with baking paper.

Lightly toast the sesame seeds in a dry pan until barely browned. Place on a wide plate and mix with the syrup until sticky.

Slice the pistachios or chop them and place on a wide plate.

When ready to shape, take a portion of the dough and roll it into a rope about 1 cm (½ in) in diameter. Cut into pieces the size of a small glass marble. The smaller the pieces are, the thinner you can press them, and the crunchier they will be. Roll the dough pieces into balls and lightly press into the pistachios for a few to stick. Remove and flip the other sides into the sesame mixture and press with your fingers to flatten and cover that side. The traditional cookies are just 1–2 mm (¹/₁₆ in) thick. Place on the baking sheet, sesame-side up. The cookies can be placed close to one another since they don't expand much.

Bake for 10–12 minutes until golden brown. Cool and store in an airtight container for up to a month.

Festiyeh

Peanut brittle bars

There is a small cart on the bank of Al Berdawni river in Zahle, one of the major cities in the Beqaa, that sells all sorts of traditional candies like malban (a Lebanese variety of Turkish delight), nougat and simple nut bars. These are made with little more than the nuts of your choice and sugar. The vendor has stacks of these sweets and they're sold as an assortment by weight. I try not to buy or make these too often because I can't stop myself going back for more. The crunch of the toasted nuts and the sweetness of the sugar makes an addictive mixture that is made even more so by adding a sprinkling of salt to take the contrast to a whole different level. Melted chocolate can be poured on top of the mixture as soon it is pressed into the pan for a chocolate-topped version.

Preheat the oven to 170°C (340°F/gas 3). Line a 900 g (2 lb) loaf tin with baking paper.

Spread the peanuts over a baking sheet and toast in the oven for around 10 minutes until lightly golden. Set aside.

Melt the sugar in a heavy-based saucepan, just shaking the pan (not stirring) until it forms a light caramel. Add the honey and salt, mix together, then add the peanuts and mix to incorporate. Transfer to the loaf tin and press until it forms a block. (Alternatively, you can just press it between 2 sheets of baking paper until it forms an even block.) Allow to cool slightly.

While the mixture is still warm, cut the block into bars or bite-sized pieces with a sharp knife. Leave to harden completely (this may take an hour or two). Wrap in baking paper or waxed paper and store in an airtight container away from humidity for up to a week.

*MAKES ABOUT 10–12 BARS
OR 20–24 BITE-SIZED PIECES*

250 g (generous 1½ cups) peanuts
120 g (generous ½ cup) white
　granulated sugar
2 tablespoons honey
½ teaspoon salt

Sfouf

Turmeric cake

A recipe that reminds me of Lent, since it contains no dairy or animal products. I still dream of the sfouf tray that our neighbour Zakiye brought us once. Typically, this golden sheet cake is light and crumbly, but Zakiye made it moist and slightly dense. To achieve that, you can increase the sugar quantity to give it moisture, add more oil to prevent it from drying out, and it is also said that a little milk can make the cake softer. This recipe makes a balanced cake, which can hold its shape, is a little moist, and is definitely one you will be making again and again.

Preheat the oven to 180°C (350°F/gas 4).

Combine the semolina, flour, sugar, turmeric and baking powder in a mixing bowl.

If using ground aniseed: mix it in with the dry ingredients, then add the water and oil and mix well.

If using whole aniseeds: bring the measured water to the boil in a saucepan, add the seeds and boil for 5 minutes. Strain out the seeds, reserving the water (add more water to ensure you have 250 ml/1 cup, if needed) and add it to the dry ingredients along with the oil. Mix well.

Prepare a 25 cm (10 in) square baking tin (or similar) by greasing the sides with the tahini. Pour in the batter mixture and sprinkle the top with the sesame seeds.

Bake for 20 minutes, or until set and a toothpick comes out clean when inserted into the middle of the sponge.

Leave to cool in the tin, then cut it into squares or diamond shapes. Store in an airtight container for up to a week.

MAKES ABOUT 20 PIECES

360 g (scant 3 cups) fine semolina
100 g (⅔ cup) plain (all-purpose) flour
250 g (generous 1 cup) white granulated sugar
1 tablespoon ground turmeric
2 teaspoons baking powder
1 tablespoon ground aniseed
  (or 2 tablespoons whole aniseeds)
250 ml (1 cup) water
125 ml (½ cup) vegetable oil
2 tablespoons tahini
40 g (¼ cup) sesame seeds (or pine nuts or blanched almonds)

Sfouf bi Debes

Carob molasses cake

Sfouf bi debes *is a variation on the regular* sfouf *recipe. Debes is molasses and this recipe is made with carob molasses, which is made by crushing and fermenting carob pods, then squeezing the liquid out and boiling it to a thick, syrupy consistency. Carob has an earthy cocoa flavour and is incredibly sweet, so it replaces the sugar in this recipe and gives a softer texture to the cake.*

Preheat the oven to 180°C (350°F/gas 4).

Combine the semolina, flour and baking powder in a mixing bowl.

If using ground aniseed: mix it in with the dry ingredients, then add the water, oil and molasses and mix well.

If using whole aniseeds: bring the measured water to the boil in a saucepan, add the seeds and boil for 5 minutes. Strain out the seeds, reserving the water (add more water to ensure you have 250 ml/1 cup, if needed) and add it to the dry ingredients along with the oil and molasses. Mix well.

Prepare a 25 cm (10 in) square baking tin (or similar) by greasing the sides with tahini. Pour in the batter mixture and sprinkle the top with the pine nuts.

Bake for 20 minutes, or until set and a toothpick comes out clean when inserted into the middle of the sponge. I like to keep this cake moist so I under-bake it a little.

Leave to cool in the tin, then cut it into squares or diamond shapes. Store in an airtight container for up to a week.

MAKES ABOUT 20 PIECES

360 g (scant 3 cups) fine semolina
100 g (⅔ cup) plain (all-purpose) flour
2 teaspoons baking powder
1 tablespoon ground aniseed
  (or 2 tablespoons whole aniseeds)
250 ml (1 cup) water
125 ml (½ cup) vegetable oil
250 ml (1 cup) carob molasses
  (or other thick molasses)
2 tablespoons tahini
20 g (2 tablespoons) pine nuts

Fôret Noire

Lebanese-style Black Forest cake

It was not a good birthday party if there wasn't a Lebanese Fôret Noire *cake. The star of the table has always been this cake. Not to be confused with German Black Forest gateau, the Lebanese version features no kirsch or black cherries. It is made with tinned fruit cocktail and the syrup from the tin moistens the sponge layers. The cake is usually covered in whipped cream and chocolate vermicelli or chocolate shavings and is sometimes topped with strawberries, if available. You will find this version on sale in most Lebanese pastry shops – only a few high-end or international patisseries make the cake with cherries, and very few with kirsch.*

Preheat the oven to 180°C (350°F/gas 4). Grease two 20 cm (8 in) round cake tins with the oil or butter and line the bases with baking paper.

Sift together the flour and cocoa powder in a large bowl. Sprinkle a little of the mixture over the sides of the cake tins and tap out any excess.

In a separate bowl, use an electric beater to beat the egg yolks with half of the sugar until fluffy and pale, around 4 minutes. Stir in a quarter of the flour mixture, then beat until incorporated. Repeat to add the rest of the flour, a quarter at a time. Add the baking powder, vanilla and salt and mix well.

In a clean bowl with a clean whisk, beat the egg whites with the remaining sugar to stiff peaks. Take a large spoonful of the whipped egg whites and mix into the cake batter until incorporated. Gently fold in half of the remaining egg whites, then add the final half and fold until well incorporated, trying not to lose too much air. Divide the cake batter between the prepared cake tins.

Bake in the middle of the oven for 12–15 minutes, or until an inserted toothpick comes out clean. Don't open the oven for the first 10 minutes, otherwise the cake might collapse. Remove from the oven and leave to cool completely.

Meanwhile, drain the tinned fruit, reserving the syrup. Whip the cream with the sugar until stiff and refrigerate until needed.

Once cooled, cut each cake into 2 layers. Place one layer on a serving plate and brush with some of the fruit syrup. Top with a quarter of the whipped cream and a third of the tinned fruit. Repeat with the other cake layers, finishing with a bottom layer of sponge so that you have a flat surface on top. Cover with the last of the cream and sprinkle with chocolate vermicelli or grated chocolate. Refrigerate before serving.

SERVES 6–8

2 teaspoons vegetable oil or butter, for greasing
120 g (¾ cup) plain (all-purpose) flour
30 g (¼ cup) unsweetened cocoa powder
7 eggs, separated
120 g (½ cup) caster (superfine) sugar
1 teaspoon baking powder
1 teaspoon vanilla extract
¼ teaspoon salt

TO FINISH
1 × 450 g (1 lb) tin of fruit cocktail in syrup
250 ml (1 cup) whipping cream
60 g (¼ cup) caster (superfine) sugar
100 g (3½ oz) dark chocolate vermicelli or grated dark chocolate

Qizha

Palestinian black cake

Qizha is the Palestinian name for nigella seeds from which a thick paste is made (also known as black sesame tahini). This paste is what makes this cake and gives it both the black colour and a sharp, slightly bitter flavour. It is said that nigella seeds have many health benefits, which explains their Arabic name, habbet al barake, *which translates to "the seed of blessing". I was first introduced to this unique recipe in the old souk of Saida, which has a mix of Palestinian and Lebanese cultures since there are many refugees who live there. There is a baker in the souk who is famous both for his* lahm baajine *(see page 56) and his trays of qizha decorated with almonds. On my first try, I was overwhelmed by the crumbly texture and the bitter taste, but I grew to like it more and more. For this recipe, I adjusted it to fit the taste of my family and friends who felt that the qizha from Saida was too bitter. This one was perfect for them – they loved it.*

Qizha can be tricky to buy, so you could substitute it for regular tahini, which will make a paler cake with a slightly less bitter flavour.

MAKES ABOUT 30 PIECES

170 g (1⅓ cups) fine semolina
140 g (scant 1 cup) plain flour
170 g (¾ cup) caster (superfine) sugar
30 g (4 tablespoons) cocoa powder
24 g (3 tablespoons) sesame seeds
1 teaspoon baking powder
pinch of salt
60 ml (¼ cup) olive oil
130 g (scant ½ cup) qizha (black sesame tahini/nigella seed paste)
150–200 ml (scant ⅔–generous ¾ cup) warm water
1 tablespoon tahini

TO FINISH

20 g (about 30) blanched almonds
125 ml (½ cup) light simple syrup (page 103)

Preheat the oven to 180°C (350°F/gas 4).

Soak the almonds for decorating in warm water and set aside.

In a large bowl, mix all of the dry ingredients. Add the liquid ingredients, starting with the 150 ml (scant ⅔ cup) of water, and mix until incorporated. You are looking for a thick batter, somewhere between a cookie batter and brownie batter. You might need to add more water (around 50 ml/scant ¼ cup) to achieve this.

Coat the bottom of a 25 cm (10 in) round cake pan with the tablespoon of tahini, then add the batter and spread to form an even layer.

Drain the almonds, then arrange them in a grid pattern on top of the batter.

Bake for 30 minutes. Once baked, remove from the oven and generously brush the top of the cake with the light simple syrup. Leave to cool in the tin.

Cut into diamond shapes and serve. Store in an airtight container for up to 2 weeks.

Burnt Basque Baklava Cheesecake

The San Sebastián (or burnt Basque) cheesecake has reached restaurants and cafés in Lebanon now and it's very popular. I thought of giving it an eastern Mediterranean twist with a baklava crust of pistachios and rose water, but otherwise have kept it quite simple. I often use labneh in sweet dishes – it's creamy with a little bit of tang and I prefer that to the usual cream cheese.

Line the base and sides of a 24 cm (9½ in) round cake pan or springform pan with 2 large layers of baking paper, large enough to go over the top of the pan. This will help release the cheesecake from the bottom and sides of the pan. Spread a thin layer of the melted butter over the paper.

Prepare the pistachio filling by pulsing the pistachios in a food processor with the sugar to a coarse crumble. Add the orange blossom water and mix with a spoon.

Divide the pile of filo sheets into 4 equal piles and keep covered with a damp cloth while you work. Take the first portion of pastry sheets and add each layer to the cake pan, letting the pastry sheets climb the sides of the pan and brushing a little butter in between each filo sheet. Once you have finished layering the first pile of filo sheets, spread a third of the pistachio filling on top. Add the second portion of the pastry sheets, brushing with butter between each filo sheet in the same way, then cover with another third of the pistachio filling. Repeat with the third portion of pastry sheets and the last portion of the pistachio filling. Top with the last pile of pastry sheets and brush the remaining butter over the top. Set aside.

For the cheesecake filling, pound the mastic with a little bit of the sugar.

In a large bowl, cream the labneh and remaining sugar with the mastic sugar. Add the eggs, floral waters and flour and beat until incorporated. Pour the mixture into the pan on top of the pastry.

Preheat the oven to 220°C (430°F/gas 7) – ideally do not use the fan setting for this style of cheesecake.

Bake the cheesecake for 40–45 minutes until the filling is a little jiggly in the centre but not too runny. Remove from the oven and let cool completely before releasing from the pan. It will be even better if you refrigerate it once it cools before cutting into it.

Decorate with dehydrated orange slices or candied oranges and pistachios. Drizzle with simple syrup or your favourite lemon or orange syrup for extra sweetness, if you like.

SERVES 8–10

100 g (3½ oz) butter, melted

200 g (7 oz) filo (phyllo) pastry sheets

dehydrated orange slices or candied oranges, to decorate

regular simple syrup (page 103) (or orange or lemon syrup), to drizzle (optional)

FOR THE PISTACHIO FILLING

150 g (1 cup) pistachios, plus extra (optional) to decorate

30 g (2 tablespoons) white granulated sugar

1 tablespoon orange blossom water

FOR THE CHEESECAKE FILLING

7 pieces of mastic (total size of a green pea)

220 g (1 cup) white granulated sugar

500 g (2 cups) labneh

5 eggs

1 tablespoon rose water (or more to taste)

1 tablespoon orange blossom water (or more to taste)

2 tablespoons plain (all-purpose) flour

Arabic Coffee, Date & Cardamom Cake

Here is another confusing part of our culture: coffee is coffee, but Arabic coffee comes from the Arabian peninsula and is boiled with lots of cardamom, while the style of coffee most commonly known in the eastern Mediterranean is Turkish-style coffee (but sometimes we call it Lebanese coffee) and it can sometimes have a hint of cardamom. This is not a point of argument since you can adjust the intensity of the coffee and cardamom in this cake to your liking. Infusing the caramel with cardamom intensifies the flavour even further.

MAKES ABOUT 15 PIECES

1–2 tablespoons tahini

250 ml (1 cup) water

2–3 tablespoons Arabic coffee (or finely ground espresso), adjust depending on how strong you want the coffee flavour to be

seeds of 5 cardamom pods

300 g (10½ oz) pitted dates (or date paste)

1 teaspoon bicarbonate of soda (baking soda)

50 ml (1¾ fl oz) carob molasses (or any other dark molasses)

2 eggs

75 ml (2½ fl oz) olive oil

1 teaspoon baking powder

1 teaspoon fine salt

2 teaspoons ground ginger

200 g (1⅔ cups) plain (all-purpose) flour

FOR THE CARAMEL POURING SAUCE

seeds from 2 cardamom pods

125 ml (½ cup) full-fat (whole) milk

250 g (1⅓ cups) brown sugar

75 g (2¾ oz) butter

1 teaspoon fine salt

Preheat the oven to 180°C (350°F/Gas 4). Prepare a 20 cm (8 in) round or 23 cm (9 in) square cake pan by coating the bottom and sides with tahini.

Bring the measured water to the boil in a small saucepan. Add the coffee and stir, then bring back to the boil. Stir again, bring back to the boil a final time, then remove from the heat.

Pound the cardamom to a fine powder (or pulse in a spice grinder with a teaspoon of sugar if needed to help it grind better), add it to the coffee and stir. Leave to stand for 5 minutes for the coffee grounds to settle to the bottom.

Place the pitted dates or date paste in a bowl along with the bicarbonate of soda. Strain the warm coffee over and leave to stand for 5 minutes.

Add the molasses, eggs and oil to the date mixture and mix until incorporated (it helps to blend with a stick blender – or in a food processor – to make the mix smooth enough). Add all the dry ingredients and stir to incorporate.

Pour the batter into the cake pan and bake for 30 minutes, or until an inserted skewer comes out clean. Remove from the oven and leave to cool slightly.

To prepare the caramel, get all your ingredients ready before you start. You should never leave caramel on the stove out of sight. Pound or blend the cardamom seeds and sift to remove any large bits. Warm the milk slightly (1 minute in the microwave is fine).

Place the sugar in a wide, heavy-based saucepan over a high heat. Once you see some sugar melting, reduce the heat to medium and wait until most of the sugar has melted. Stir until there are no lumps. Add the butter and whisk until combined (be careful as it might bubble and steam). Add the milk and whisk until incorporated (again, take care). Heat for 1 more minute, then remove from the heat, add the salt and cardamom powder and pour into a jug.

Serve slices of the cake warm, or reheated, with the warm caramel drizzled over the top.

Aish el Saraya
x Layali Loubnan

Semolina and *ashta* 'cheesecake'

This recipe is a sort of mash-up between aish el saraya *(a syrup-soaked bread base topped with* ashta *and nuts),* madlouka *(a dessert similar to Mafrouke, page 126) and* layali Loubnan *(semolina pudding) in the form of a cheesecake. Most* aish el saraya *recipes are made with old bread or toasted sandwich bread, but I find it tiresome to get fresh bread and toast it or wait for it to become stale whenever I want to eat this. For this reason, some people make it with cooked semolina, which takes it into* madlouka *and* layali Loubnan *territory. Here, the cooked semolina is given colour and flavour from the caramelised sugar. It makes a pretty centrepiece dessert topped with rose petals. You can serve this as individual cheesecakes or make one large cheesecake you can slice into – it's up to you.*

Add the semolina to a large saucepan along with half of the butter and cook over a medium heat until lightly coloured and fragrant. Remove to a bowl and set aside.

To the same pan, add 25 g (2 tablespoons) of the sugar and allow it to melt and caramelise to the colour you desire. Alternatively, you can caramelise all of the sugar instead of just a portion and the resulting colour of the dessert will be darker. Once the sugar has caramelised, add the remaining butter and stir until incorporated. Add the warm water, the remaining 50 g (¼ cup) sugar (if not already used) and the orange blossom water along with the semolina. Stir over a medium heat until the semolina is cooked and soft (adding small amounts of extra water, if needed).

Place a 15 cm (6 in) ring mould on a small dessert plate. Press a quarter or a fifth of the semolina mixture (depending on how many you are serving) into the ring mould to form a flat layer (you can press it along the sides as well like a cheesecake). Top with the *ashta*, then decorate with ground pistachios and rose petals. Repeat to make 4–5 plated desserts. Alternatively, make one large cheesecake in a 23 cm (9 in) springform pan. Allow to cool completely, then chill thoroughly in the refrigerator before unmoulding.

Serve cold with rose jam or simple syrup to sweeten.

*SERVES 4–5 AS INDIVIDUAL PORTIONS
(OR UP TO 8 IF MAKING LARGE
VERSION)*

125 g (scant 1 cup) coarse semolina
20 g (¾ oz) butter
75 g (⅓ cup) white granulated sugar
250 ml (1 cup) warm water
1 tablespoon orange blossom water
250 g (9 oz) *Ashta* (page 102)
50 g (⅓ cup) ground pistachios
10 g (¼ oz) edible rose petals

TO SERVE

rose jam or simple syrup
   (page 103), to taste

Sweets & Desserts

Sweets are equally as important as savoury foods in our culture, they complete a meal. A spread of sweets is laid on the table once the food is lifted. Expect to be served semolina cakes, puddings, *Ashta* (page 102) and seasonal fruits. Sweets also make up the afternoon *asrouniye* (teatime) spread, with coffee or tea in winter, or fresh juices, lemonade or homemade fruit syrup drinks in summer. Guests invited for lunch or dinner or *iftar* (the meal that marks the end of a fasting day) are expected to show up with some sort of sweet. Whether it is a homemade baked good or sweets or a store-bought item, it is considered rude to show up without something for the host or the party – unless it's a casual gathering of friends, but even then we still ask if we're expected to make or bring something.

We grew up with my mom making a lot of desserts at home. She made puddings and *Knafe* (page 121) and *Atayef* (filled pancakes, a recipe for this is in my first book), as well as pancakes, crêpes and sponge cakes. She loves to try new stuff and she introduced us to a lot of things until we grew up and started bringing home recipes or sweets that were new to her. You will find many of our family favourites in this chapter.

Our sweets repertoire in the East Mediterranean (or West Asia) has influences that reach across borders. The lack of proper documentation makes finding the origins of old recipes a near impossible task. Recipes travel and evolve, some originated from this part of the world, while some come from further away, and some even travelled abroad, changing and evolving, only to return home to eclipse the older local versions. For the sweet recipes in this chapter, I used versions that are now commonly made in our region, in Lebanon, Palestine and Syria. Similar recipes can be found in Turkish cuisine – with the exchange happening during or after the Ottoman Empire's mandate over the region – and in Greek and Cypriot cuisines.

A comment that is often heard when talking about East Mediterranean sweets is that they're way too sweet (similarities are often drawn to Greek and Turkish sweets, especially when syrup is drizzled on top of the confectionery or when they're dipped in it). An overlooked detail is that our confectioneries contain no or very little sugar in themselves - they are sweetened afterwards by the use of syrup. This means that the sweetness level can be controlled. I've observed that when I try to make recipes from foreign (often American) cookbooks or blogs, I find I have to cut the sugar amount almost in half for it to reach a sweetness level I like. In the recipes I make, I try to cut down on amounts of sugar I find to be excessive (but of course, I keep it where it is necessary for the recipe to work). Feel free to use more sweetener to your own liking.

Tarboosh

Chocolate-coated meringue kisses

Controversy surrounds this simple recipe of chocolate-covered meringue on a biscuit base because of its name. Tarboosh (meaning "fez") is the replacement name that Gandour, the manufacturer, used to rebrand the treat. The former name (used both in the Middle East and in several European countries in less enlightened times) was the derogatory racial allusion ras al abed *(meaning "head of the slave"). Originating in Denmark, there are variants of this recipe to be found the world over, and it remains a very popular treat in Lebanon.*

This version is made with egg whites, but it could also be made with soapwort root (see page 139) for a more shelf-stable version.

In a large bowl, beat the egg whites and lemon juice with an electric beater to stiff peaks.

Combine the sugar and water in a small pan over a medium heat. Bring to the boil, gently stirring for around 10 minutes, or until it reaches 115°C (240°F).

Pour the syrup in a thin stream over the whipped egg whites while beating continuously until it is all incorporated and the mixture turns glossy. Mix in the vanilla extract. Scoop into a piping bag or ziplock bag with the corner snipped off and pipe the marshmallow mixture onto the wafers or biscuits in a large pile. Place on a tray lined with baking paper and refrigerate for 30 minutes.

Melt three-quarters of the chocolate by microwaving it for 20-second intervals until softened. Alternatively, melt the chocolate in a bain marie to 45°C (113°F). Make sure no water or any other liquid gets into the melted chocolate. Mix off the heat until all the chocolate is combined, then add the remaining chocolate and stir in until completely melted. This should cool it to 26°C (79°F). Reheat either on the bain marie or in the microwave in short bursts to 32°C (90°F). This will temper the chocolate to make it harden quicker, snap when bitten into, and be less prone to melting. If you don't have a thermometer, do the same steps while keeping in mind not to heat the chocolate too much, bringing the temperature back up to something close to your body temperature.

If you're dipping the biscuits into the melted chocolate, take each piece and dip it head first until completely covered. Add a teaspoon of the chocolate to the baking paper-lined tray and place the biscuit directly on it. Fill in any gaps by spreading the chocolate with a toothpick and adding more when needed. Alternatively, drizzle the melted chocolate on top of each biscuit in a spiral fashion for a fun look. Refrigerate until set.

Serve cold, or at room temperature, ideally on the day of making.

MAKES 15

3 egg whites (around 100 g/3½ oz)

2 tablespoons lemon juice

190 g (generous ¾ cup) white granulated sugar

60 ml (¼ cup) water

2 teaspoons vanilla extract

15 round wafers or Marie biscuits

400 g (14 oz) dark chocolate (or a mix of dark and milk chocolate)

Mammouniye

Syrian semolina pudding

This is probably one of the easiest and quickest recipes in this book. A simple porridge for a filling breakfast on a cold morning, this Syrian dessert is still made in Aleppo on Fridays (the end of the week in some Muslim-majority countries), along with Shaabiyat (page 110) on major holidays and celebrations. It is thought that the name comes from al-Ma'mun, the seventh Abbasid Caliph in the ninth century. However, Khayr al-Din al-Asadi, a Syrian historian, disputes this, as in all of the Caliph's documented life there was no mention of this dish. In his Comparative Encyclopedia of Aleppo, al-Asadi suggests that the dish was named for its original maker, a man named Maamoun from the Souq Al Saqatiya in Aleppo, although he doesn't state a date or period.

I learned about this recipe from a guest chef who visited the restaurant I was working at in 2016 and I have been making it ever since. I recommend using Czech Akkawi Cheese, Majdouli or Mshallale, or even Nabulsi cheese, rinsed to remove excess salt to your taste. Alternatively, mozzarella could work for a similar texture.

SERVES 6

50 g (1¾ oz) butter

150 g (1 cup) coarse semolina

220 g (1 cup) white granulated sugar

1 litre (4 cups) water

2 teaspoons ground cinnamon, plus extra to serve

100–150 g (3½–5 oz) Czech Akkawi, Nabulsi or Mshallale cheese (string cheese), rinsed to remove salt, to taste

50 g (⅓ cup) ground pistachios

simple syrup (page 103), to serve (optional)

In a large saucepan, melt the butter, then add the semolina and toast until golden. Add the sugar and water and stir over a medium-low heat until the water has been absorbed and the semolina is cooked and soft. Add the cinnamon and a third of the cheese and stir to incorporate.

To serve, divide the mixture among 6 bowls and top each with another sprinkling of cinnamon. Shred the remaining cheese and divide among the bowls, then top with the ground pistachios. Serve drizzled with some simple syrup if more sweetness is needed.

Mshabbak

Sweet lavender fritters

The name of this sweet literally translates to "tangled" for the shape they are made in. These crunchy, fried treats are traditionally half-dipped in red food colouring to create a unique look that contrasts with their natural yellow hue. I think of them as the cousin of the funnel cake and Indian jalebi that have had a slight makeover. It's fascinating the endless possibilities of confectionery that you can make with just some flour and water. This recipe makes a thin mshabbak that remains crunchy and isn't a complete sugar bomb.

Prepare the syrup first as it needs to be completely cold before using. Place the beetroot in a small saucepan with the water and boil until reduced by half. Strain, add the sugar and lavender, then bring to the boil and cook until all the sugar is dissolved and the liquid is clear. Add the lemon juice and remove from the heat. Strain again, leave to cool, then refrigerate before using.

In a large bowl, mix together the flour, cornflour, baking powder and salt.

Pound the lemon zest, lavender and sugar together in a pestle and mortar to infuse the sugar with the fragrant oils. At this point you can sift it to remove the lavender flowers or use as is. Add the sugar to the flour mixture, then gradually add the water until the mixture is thick and will slowly drip off of the spoon or spatula.

Pour the batter mixture into a squeezy bottle or a piping bag fitted with a thin nozzle. Pour the cold syrup into a wide plate or pan and set nearby.

Heat the oil for deep-frying in a small, deep pan over a medium-low heat.

When the oil is hot enough for frying, squeeze the batter into the oil in the form of small spiralling loops until you have formed a disc the size of a teacup saucer. You can make them bigger if desired. Fry for 1 minute until slightly set, then flip with a slotted spoon and fry for 30 seconds more, avoiding browning the dough.

Remove to drain on a wire rack (or form a makeshift rack with chopsticks on a plate) and let cool for 30 seconds before dunking into the cold syrup for 30 seconds. Remove them quicker if they are absorbing too much syrup and falling apart, but if they're thin they should be crispy and will take on as much syrup as needed. Leave them in for longer, or double dip, to thicken the glaze. Set again on the rack to drain of excess syrup.

Serve immediately or store in an airtight container where they will keep for about 2 days.

MAKES AROUND 10

75 g (½ cup) plain (all-purpose) flour
60 g (½ cup) cornflour (cornstarch)
½ teaspoon baking powder
½ teaspoon fine salt
zest of 1 lemon
1 tablespoon lavender flowers
2 tablespoons caster (superfine) sugar
125 ml (½ cup) water
neutral oil, for deep-frying

FOR THE SYRUP

1 beetroot (beet) (around 150 g/5 oz), peeled and roughly diced
250 ml (1 cup) water
230 g (1 cup) caster (superfine) sugar
1 tablespoon lavender flowers
1 teaspoon lemon juice

Maakroun

Fried aniseed finger doughnuts

Maakroun, Mshabbak (*page 173*) *and* Awaymet (*page 179*) *are an inseparable trio on saints' holidays and are among the recipes traditionally prepared for Saint Barbara's Day, along with* Ameh (*page 184*) *and atayef (a recipe I share in my first book, Bayrut). Sweet shacks line the streets next to churches, the ones celebrating the saint of the day, with their iconic red-and-white-striped awnings and stacks of sweets in large aluminium trays creating an almost psychedelic vision of colours, shapes and light. The selection has grown over the years to include more sweets to try to capture more clients.*

Maakroun are my favourite holiday sweets. Flavoured with aniseed and soaked in a thick syrup, they have a consistency similar to cake pops and crumble when you bite into them.

MAKES AROUND 25

2 tablespoons whole aniseeds
  (or 2–3 teaspoons ground aniseed)
350–375 ml (1⅓–1½ cups) water
140 g (scant 1 cup) plain (all-purpose) flour
100 g (generous ¾ cup) fine semolina
½ teaspoon salt
½ teaspoon dried instant yeast
60 ml (¼ cup) vegetable oil, plus extra for deep-frying

FOR THE SYRUP

440 g (2 cups) white granulated sugar
125 ml (½ cup) water
1 teaspoon lemon juice
  (or a dash of citric acid)

Prepare the syrup first by mixing the sugar and water in a saucepan. Bring to the boil and allow to simmer until the sugar has melted and the syrup is clear, around 3–5 minutes. Add the lemon juice (or citric acid) to prevent crystallisation. Set aside to cool. It must be cold before using.

If using whole aniseeds, infuse the measured water by adding the aniseeds to it in a saucepan and simmering for 5 minutes. If using ground aniseeds, skip this step. Let the water cool to room temperature.

Mix the flour and semolina in a bowl, then add the salt and yeast on opposite sides of the bowl. Add the ground aniseeds (if using) and pour in the measured vegetable oil. Mix until the mixture looks like wet sand. Pour in half the liquid (water or aniseed infusion) and mix until it has been absorbed. Add more as needed to reach a dough-like consistency that you can hold and shape in your hand.

Take small pieces of dough (about the size of a ping pong ball) and mould to the shape of a date. Place on the side of a large-holed grater and press gently with the tips of your fingers while moving the ball of dough slightly down the grater to create a raised pattern of spikes. You can also use the same technique with a fork or gnocchi board or on a strainer – anything with multiple holes that will give shape to the dough.

Heat the oil for deep-frying in a small, deep pan over a medium-low heat. When the oil is hot enough, add the *maakroun* and fry until golden brown (you may need to do this in batches). Use a slotted spoon or metal tongs to remove the *maakroun* from the oil and dunk into the cold syrup for 30 seconds, then remove to a plate or container.

Test the inside texture of one and adjust the soaking time in the syrup to your liking. Leaving it for less time will coat the outside layer only, while leaving it in longer will create a dense and crumbly *maakroun* with a good sugary kick. Find the sweet spot that works for you. Store in an airtight container and consume within 2–3 days.

Awaymet Maa Zanjabeel

Ginger doughnut balls in fig-leaf syrup

Doughnuts are not uniquely a Lebanese or Palestinian recipe, but in the Arabian Peninsula, they are also called lugeimat, luqaimat, *or* loqmet al qadi *("the judge's bites") for their small size and the fact that they can be eaten in one whole bite. The dough must be runny and the double-frying method is crucial for better browning and crunch. The syrup must also be cold to create the thermal shock that will help the doughnuts to absorb the syrup but maintain the crunch. Don't make them a long time in advance, and only make enough to serve on the same day, as their texture doesn't hold for long.*

I decided to spice these up a bit from the traditional recipe by adding fresh ginger, which add a nice sharp kick to the dough, and infusing the syrup with fig leaf, which adds a coconutty fragrance. Feel free to omit either or both if they're not available or if you prefer to stick to the classic flavour. Or make both the dough and syrup with fresh ginger for extra-gingery doughnuts.

MAKES AROUND 30

FOR THE DOUGH

140 g (scant 1 cup) plain (all-purpose) flour

½ teaspoon dried instant yeast

1 teaspoon white granulated sugar

150 ml (generous ½ cup) ginger-infused water or plain water

small knob of fresh root ginger (about 12 g/¼ oz), grated

FOR THE SYRUP

500 g (2¼ cups) white granulated sugar

250 ml (1 cup) water

1 teaspoon lemon juice

5 fig leaves, cut into pieces

neutral oil, for deep-frying

In a large bowl or a stand mixer fitted with a dough hook, mix all the dough ingredients until you have a smooth and elastic dough. Cover and set aside to rise for around 30 minutes.

Prepare the syrup by combining the sugar and water in a medium saucepan over a medium heat. Once the sugar has dissolved, add the lemon juice and fig leaves and simmer in the sugar syrup for 5 minutes. Strain and leave to cool.

Once the dough is ready, transfer it to a piping bag and cut off a wide tip. Use this to pipe the dough into small balls about the size of a ping pong ball. Alternatively, you can use 2 oiled spoons to portion the dough into balls, re-oiling them between each shaping. Another method for shaping the balls is to squeeze off bits of dough in your fist and use an oiled spoon to snip them off and shape.

Heat enough oil for deep-frying in a deep-sided, heavy frying pan to 180–190°C (350–375°F).

Take each dough ball and drop it into the frying oil (you will need to work in batches). Fry until light golden and bobbing up to the surface, then remove with a slotted spoon to a colander. Continue until all of the dough is shaped and fried.

Fry all the balls for a second time until well browned, then remove with a slotted spoon straight into the cooled syrup. Carefully stir to coat, then remove to a plate to cool before serving. Best eaten on the day of making.

Riz Bhalib

Aromatic rice pudding

This is a classic dessert that is common to have in most restaurants – even the takeaway sandwich shops serve it, along with strawberry or cherry jelly and custard, in small plastic cups. I enjoy the riz bhalib *we make at home as it really hits the spot with the aromatics we use and a texture that is not too firm and not runny. At home we usually serve it on its own, but I prefer to reduce the sweetness in the mix itself and use either fruit jam or stewed fruits to top it. I was cooking this once at a supper club and kept calling it "rice pudding" until my friend told me I had fooled her and made her think it was some fancy dessert when it was plain old* riz bhalib. *You can serve it as unadorned or as fancy as you like with fruit jam and crushed nuts.*

SERVES 6

250 g (generous 1 cup) short-grain rice
750 ml (3 cups) water
500 ml (2 cups) milk
3 pieces of mastic
4 tablespoons white granulated sugar
1 tablespoon rose water
1 tablespoon orange blossom water
30 g (3 tablespoons) whole almonds
30 g (⅓ cup) walnuts
60 g (3 tablespoons) fig jam, or jam of your preference.

Soak the rice in the measured water for 1–2 hours.

Place the rice with its soaking water in a large saucepan and bring to the boil, then reduce the heat, cover and cook for 15 minutes, stirring once or twice to make sure it isn't sticking to the pan. Once most of the water has been absorbed or the bottom of the mixture is starting to dry out, add the milk and stir to combine.

Grind the mastic with a little bit of the sugar in a pestle and mortar, then add the mixture to the pan with the remaining sugar and stir. Bring to the boil and cook for 5 minutes while stirring.

Remove from the heat and leave to cool for around 10 minutes before adding the rose water and orange blossom water. Scoop the mixture into bowls, cover and leave to cool.

Crush, chop or process the almonds and walnuts to your preferred consistency. Serve the puddings sprinkled with the crunchy nuts along with a spoonful of jam.

Cocktail Fweke She'af

Fruit cocktail with avocado and strawberry purées

SERVES 4

FOR THE AVOCADO PURÉE

400 g (14 oz) avocado flesh

100 ml (generous ⅓ cup) water or milk
(or more as needed)

FOR THE STRAWBERRY PURÉE

300 g (10½ oz) strawberries

100 ml (generous ⅓ cup) water or milk
(or more as needed)

FOR THE COCKTAIL

2 medium bananas (160 g/5½ oz)

¼ mango (180 g/6½ oz)

1 apple (100 g/3½ oz)

other fruits of choice: kiwi,
pineapple, melon etc.

225 g (1 cup) *Ashta* (page 102)

4 tablespoons honey

100 g (3½ oz) nuts (cashews, almonds,
pistachios, pine nuts), soaked in water
and drained

extra fruit pieces, to decorate

There are certain blessings that we often overlook due to their uninterrupted availability. We never used to make fruit cocktails at home. We would make a fruit salad but never this fruit cocktail. This treat was reserved for a visit to Al Antabli, a well-known fruit cocktail and sweet shop in the coastal town of Tabarja. In the glory days of Lebanon, this shop had an iconic branch in the heart of the old souk in Al Balad, a main attraction in the capital Beirut. After the 1975–1990 civil war, the whole area was bought by a private company linked to a high-ranking businessman who transformed it into a luxury souk with no soul. Al Antabli opened there again with its iconic fountain, yet the whole area was abandoned after a series of devastating events, including violent clashes between protestors and the army and police, the pandemic, the harbour explosion and the economic crisis. Plans to revive the area have always flopped because we collectively never identified with the revamped area that no longer felt like Al Balad. So, this is our recipe for a homemade fruit cocktail like Al Antabli would make.

Blend the avocado with a little bit of water or milk into a smooth purée that's slightly runny (start with 100 ml/generous ⅓ cup and add more to thin it out, if needed).

Purée the strawberries the same way, reserving a few whole ones to build the cocktails.

Peel and chop the fruits into small 1–1.5 cm (½ in) pieces. Layer the fruits in half-pint glasses (or any large, clear dishes), adding the sliced bananas first, then the strawberries. Fill each glass to the halfway point with avocado purée, then add the rest of the fruits and top with the strawberry purée. Top with *ashta*, drizzles of honey, nuts and more fruit pieces to decorate.

Serve immediately.

Ameh Berbara

Wheat pudding

To celebrate Saint Barbara's day, the main sweet item we make is ameh (wheat) which is symbolic of the wheat field in which the saint hid when escaping persecution for adopting Christianity. The wheat is soaked, then some of it is removed and planted on a wet cotton-lined dish for Christmas celebrations. The remaining wheat is boiled with aniseed. On Saint Barbara's day, children get dressed up in disguises and visit their relatives and neighbours. My first memory of this was when we moved from the UAE to the refugee camp in Dbayeh where I have spent most of my life. I could only join the trips after I got back from school, which was around 7 pm, an hour before kids must get back home. My consolation was always the food on that day. I would be walking home from the bus and the aromas of anise for the wheat porridge and the flower extracts for the syrups would accompany me all the way.

If using whole wheat or unhulled grains, soak in water overnight. If using hulled wheat, soak for 1–2 hours.

Soak the almonds and raisins overnight in separate bowls in the refrigerator.

The next day, drain the almonds and raisins. Squeeze each almond between your fingers to remove the skin and split in half. Set aside. Tie the aniseed into a mesh bag or piece of muslin (cheesecloth).

Rinse the soaked wheat and place in a large saucepan with the measured water. Bring to the boil, then reduce the heat, add the aniseed bundle, cover and simmer for 40 minutes, or until the wheat is softened and doesn't have a tough bite anymore. Add more water, if needed – it should have a little liquid but not be wheat soup. Remove the aniseed bundle, mix in the sugar and leave to cool.

You can serve this warm or refrigerate and serve cold (it will keep in the refrigerator for up to 5 days).

When ready to serve, divide among small serving bowls and cover the whole surface of each pudding with the desiccated coconut. Decorate with the nuts and raisins and serve.

SERVES 6

250 g (1½ cups) wheat grains (whole wheat or hulled wheat)

60 g (generous ⅓ cup) whole almonds

60 g (½ cup) raisins

1 tablespoon whole aniseeds

1 litre (4 cups) water

100 g (scant ½ cup) white granulated sugar (or to taste)

60 g (⅔ cup) desiccated coconut

30 g (3 tablespoons) pine nuts

30 g (⅓ cup) walnuts

30 g (¼ cup) pistachios

Arishe w Asal

Fresh cheese with honey and fruit

Sometimes we find comfort in the simplest things. In Lebanese restaurants it is common to order the "full menu", where food just keeps coming to your table, from the salads to cold appetisers, then hot ones followed by a main dish or grilled meats. Finally, a display of sweets is laid onto the table with small coffee cups to end your meal. One often overlooked plate is the one filled with arishe, a clumpy, white cheese. Arishe is similar to cottage or ricotta cheese and is usually paired with local honey or fruit jam for sweetness. I know a restaurant, Al Shams in Anjar, that was generous enough to offer this along with fruits and sweets to all its guests at the end of their meals, regardless of whether they had ordered the lavish, often wasteful, "full menu". Simple but delicious and fresh.

Heat the milk in a large saucepan over a medium heat. Once it starts to steam, reduce the heat and add the lemon juice (or vinegar). Continue to boil until the mixture has separated and started to form curds. Gently remove the curds with a slotted spoon or a fine mesh colander to a waiting bowl. Let the milk come to the boil again and remove any more curds that might form. (The remaining whey, which should be a pale yellow colour, can be discarded or saved to be used in your next batch of bread dough instead of water or milk.) Allow the curds to cool.

SERVES 4

1 litre (4 cups) full-fat (whole) milk

2 tablespoons lemon juice
 (or white vinegar)

4 strawberries

2 bananas

honey (or jam of choice), to taste

a handful of nuts of choice (optional)

To serve, slice the strawberries and bananas. Divide the *arishe* among 4 dessert plates or bowls and top with the sliced fruit, then drizzle with 1 or 2 tablespoons of honey (or jam), according to taste. Crush the nuts (if using) and sprinkle on top. Serve immediately.

The curds can be refrigerated, covered, for 5–7 days, if ungarnished. The curds can also form the base for a simple cheese, like ricotta or cottage cheese – salt and nigella seeds can be added, then the curds pressed to shape and finally soaked in a brine to make a savoury cheese.

Roasted Nectarines

with orange blossom labneh cream, honey and pistachios

I made this once at a gathering with friends and they keep asking me to make it again. I also like to serve it at pop-ups when peaches or nectarines are in season. I prefer to make it with nectarines because I like their smooth skins and slightly tart flavour, which I like to accentuate by using slightly sour labneh with the whipped cream topping. Labneh brings a great taste and firms up the cream, which can be flavoured to one's liking. I also serve this cream over cooked cherries, or a peach or plum crumble – or just eat it with a spoon.

SERVES 8

500 ml (2 cups) double (heavy) cream

230 g (1 cup) caster (superfine) sugar

250 g (1 cup) labneh

2 tablespoons orange blossom water

1 tablespoon butter

1 kg (2 lb 4 oz) nectarines (or peaches), halved and pitted

40 g (¼ cup) pistachios, toasted and crushed

mint leaves (whole or ribboned), to decorate (optional)

a drizzle of honey, to serve

In a large bowl, whip the cream and sugar to stiff peaks. Whisk in the labneh and orange blossom water until combined. Refrigerate until needed.

Heat a griddle or frying pan until hot, add the butter and reduce the heat to low. Add the nectarines, cut sides down, and fry until lightly browned.

To serve, heap a tablespoon of the orange blossom labneh cream in the middle of each serving plate, top with a nectarine half, cut side up, and top with another heaped tablespoon of cream. Sprinkle with the crushed toasted pistachios, top with a mint leaf (ribboned if you wish), if using, and add a drizzle of honey.

Jazariye

Candied pumpkin jam with pumpkin spice

500 g (1 lb 2 oz) pumpkin flesh, skin and seeds removed

400 g (scant 2 cups) white granulated sugar

200 ml (generous ¾ cup) water

1 teaspoon lemon juice (or a small pinch of citric acid)

150 g (5 oz) mixed nuts (pine nuts, blanched almonds, cashews and pistachios)

FOR THE SPICE MIX

½ cinnamon stick

small piece of fresh nutmeg

4 cloves

small knob of fresh root ginger

4 allspice berries

FOR THE ALTERNATIVE SPICE MIX

¼–½ teaspoon of the same ground spices, to taste

OPTIONAL PICKLING LIME METHOD

50 g (1¾ oz) pickling lime (optional)

1.5 litres (6 cups) water

Despite the fact that the name refers to jazar (carrots), this sweet preserve is made with pumpkin – the name could be a reference to the shape and colour of the finished product, which resembles grated carrots. Nouh Al Haddad, the man behind Halawet el Shmayse *(page 122), displays large trays of* jazariye *in his shop. It comes in two forms: a regular jammy, sticky preserve, which can also feature nuts, or a shredded type that is more crunchy. The crunchy type is made by soaking the shredded pumpkin in pickling lime, which helps preserve the texture and prevents it from disintegrating into jam. I have suggested either way here, but the preserve made with pickling lime is certainly my favourite!*

Grate the pumpkin flesh into a saucepan and add the sugar and water. Place the spices into a muslin cloth or an infusion bag and add to the pan. (If using ground spices, add them directly to the pan.)

Bring to the boil, then reduce the heat and simmer, stirring frequently to prevent sticking and burning, until the pumpkin breaks down in the sugar mix and it thickens and comes together. This usually takes around 20 minutes.

Remove from the heat, add the lemon juice (or citric acid) and the nuts, then decant into sterilised jars. Store for up to 6 months.

If using the pickling lime method, soak the pickling lime in the measured water overnight. The next day, without disturbing the sediment, remove the clear liquid at the top and discard the sediment. Soak the grated pumpkin in the lime water overnight, then rinse very well with 3 rounds of fresh water and let the water drain. Proceed to cook the jam as instructed above.

Halawet el Smeed

Semolina pudding

Semolina is used as a base for many sweet recipes and here it is cooked into a thick, sweet paste that cools into a jiggly block. It can be used as a base for a dessert like Layali Loubnan *(page 162) if cooked with milk, or it can be topped with* Ashta *(page 102) with some syrup or jam to sweeten it further. It can also be the filling for* Tamriye *(page 192), a thin fried dough made into classic square parcels or rolled into cigars.*

MAKES ENOUGH TO FILL 12 TAMRIYE (PAGE 192)

100 g (generous ¾ cup) fine semolina

450 ml (generous 1¾ cups) water

60 g (generous ¼ cup) white granulated sugar

4 pieces of mastic plus a pinch of white granulated sugar

1 teaspoon orange blossom water

1 teaspoon rose water

Mix the semolina, water and sugar in a saucepan.

Pound the mastic and sugar to make the mastic finer, then add it to the mix in the pan. Bring to the boil while stirring continuously, then reduce the heat to medium-low and cook until the mixture thickens well.

Remove from the heat and add the aromatic waters, then pour into a bowl. Allow to cool completely before cutting into pieces as needed for your recipe.

It will keep, covered, in the refrigerator for up to 2 days.

Tamriye

Beignets filled with semolina pudding

Tamriye *and* kallaj Ramadan *are similar pastries but they are not the same. Kallaj is almost exclusively sold during Ramadan and bought fresh an hour before* iftar. *The pastries are stuffed with* Ashta *(page 102) while the similar-looking* tamriye *are filled with* Halawet el Smeed *(page 191) – a semolina pudding.* Tamriye *is one of the items sold in the shacks set in squares or next to churches during the feasts of saints. It takes skill to raise and slap the dough on the counter to spread it out as thinly as these experts do. I happened to be in Al Mrouj, a mountain village in Al Matn, during the week of the Saint Takla feast. Two shacks selling sweets were fighting for my attention when they saw me taking photos and wanted me to buy their products. I almost caused a fight between them, but I eventually tasted from both – their* tamriye *were excellent.*

Prepare the dough by mixing all the ingredients. Knead for 5 minutes until it is completely mixed and bouncy. Add some more oil to the bowl, cover and leave to rest for 20 minutes–1 hour.

Prepare the *halawet el smeed* as directed on page 191, then cut into 12 pieces.

Divide the dough into 12 balls. Work with one and return the rest to the bowl, covered, to prevent drying. Roll out on a lightly oiled surface as thin as you can. If the dough has some resistance, allow it to rest a little before stretching it again. Once stretched really thin, fold over the rough sides to form a square. Add a slice of *halawet el smeed* and fold the dough to cover by bringing in the corners towards the centre where they meet and seal shut.

Make a few, then deep-fry the prepared ones in hot oil until golden while you prepare the rest.

Drain on kitchen paper, then sprinkle with icing sugar and serve warm.

MAKES AROUND 12

250 g (1⅔ cups) plain (all-purpose) flour
170 ml (⅔ cup) water
1 tablespoon caster (superfine) sugar
1 tablespoon vegetable oil, plus extra for greasing

TO FINISH

1 × quantity of *Halawet el Smeed* (page 191)
neutral oil, for deep-frying
icing (confectioners') sugar, for dusting

Raha (Lokum)

Turkish delight

The more time goes on, the more things from my youth are starting to be considered classic. Raha and biscuits was common to have during my childhood, as a dessert and as an asrouniyeh (teatime) treat with coffee. It faded from the spotlight for a while, but for the past few years it has been having a comeback as a nostalgic favourite. I am not complaining! Raha is not quite the same as its Turkish version, lokum. Raha is supposed to be soft, so that it can be crushed and spread under the weight of two biscuits, which is how it's served. There is a shop in Saida that makes raha in different flavours, which can be done by flavouring the liquid at the start of the recipe or by using fruit juice as the base. I still prefer the traditional raha flavoured with mastic.

Add 250 g (1 cup plus 2 tablespoons) of the sugar to a small saucepan with the 175 ml (⅔ cup) water. Heat until the sugar dissolves completely, then add the citric acid and stir.

Add the cornflour slurry to the hot sugar syrup. Reduce the heat and stir immediately with a whisk until the mixture thickens really well.

If using mastic pieces, grind them with a little bit of the sugar to make them finer. Add them with the rose water and remaining sugar to the pan and stir. The mixture will loosen up a little, but keep stirring it until it starts to thicken again. Stir every other minute for around 20–25 minutes until the mixture is really thick and gooey. The mixture should start to pull away from the sides and bottom of the pan slightly and it should feel as if the mixture is searing in the pan.

Add the butter or oil and stir. This should give the mixture translucency.

Pour into a 15 cm (6 in) square container lined with oiled baking paper. Press into the container and allow it to cool completely.

Take out of the container, remove the paper and cut into about 15 pieces using a greased knife. Drop into a sealable container filled with the icing sugar and turn to coat on all sides. Store in the sealed container in the sugar and serve alongside coffee or on an *asrouniye* table squished in between two Marie biscuits.

MAKES AROUND 25 PIECES

325 g (1½ cups) white granulated sugar

175 ml (⅔ cup) water

small pinch of citric acid

75 g (scant ⅔ cup) cornflour (cornstarch) dissolved in 75 ml (⅓ cup) water

4 small pieces of mastic (optional)

1 teaspoon rose water

1 tablespoon butter or neutral oil

100–150 g (¾–1¼ cups) icing (confectioners') sugar

Al Mann w Al Salwa

Cardamom nougat with nuts

Derived from the biblical story of when God sent his people food from the sky, the other name for this confectionery is mann al sama, *which means "coming from the sky". In the story, the food was to be sent daily and was a test for people to trust in God and not store up for later days because the food would spoil. In Iraq, where this confectionery is made,* al mann *is a resin that is collected from trees before dawn when the temperature is at its lowest and the resin is in a solid state. It is then cured and used to make this chewy, cardamom-flavoured sweet treat.*

To prepare the soapwort water, wash the root well, then soak in the measured water for 12 hours. Place the mixture in a saucepan, bring to a simmer and cook until reduced by two-thirds. Strain into a jar and refrigerate. This will make more than you need, but it can be refrigerated for a week.

In a large bowl or a stand mixer fitted with a whisk, whisk the measured soapwort water for around 5 minutes until frothy and fluffy like beaten egg whites.

In a small saucepan, mix the sugar, water and honey and heat to 149°C (300°F) on a sugar thermometer, making sure it doesn't burn. Add the citric acid (or lemon juice) and carefully pour the hot sugar mixture in a thin stream over the fluffy soapwort water while whisking continuously. Keep whisking until the mixture reaches room temperature, then add the cardamom and nuts and whisk more. The mixture should stiffen up a bit.

Sprinkle half the cornflour mix into a 20 cm (8 in) square container that is 5 cm (2 in) deep and scoop the mixture into it. Cover with the remaining cornflour. Cover with cling film (plastic wrap) and refrigerate overnight.

The next day, remove the firm mixture from the cornflour and place onto a work surface dusted with cornflour. Oil a large knife and cut the nougat into 30 pieces (oiling the knife again, when needed), dusting the cut pieces with the cornflour as you go. You can store the nougat as little nuggets or roll into balls, rolling them in more cornflour to prevent sticking.

Store in an airtight container with the cornflour, away from heat and moisture (otherwise it will melt and become too sticky) for 1–2 weeks.

MAKES AROUND 30 PIECES

75 ml (⅓ cup) soapwort water (see below)

200 g (scant 1 cup) white granulated sugar

50 ml (3 tablespoons plus 1 teaspoon) water

85 g (¼ cup) honey

½ teaspoon citric acid (or 1 teaspoon lemon juice)

2 teaspoons ground cardamom

200 g (1½ cups) chopped pistachios (or half and half with walnuts)

200 g (generous 1½ cups) cornflour (cornstarch), plus extra as needed

neutral oil, for greasing

FOR THE SOAPWORT WATER

50 g (1¾ oz) soapwort root (buy online or in health food stores)

600 ml (20½ fl oz) water

Halawe Tahiniye

Tahini halva

After I discovered halawe (soapwort) root for making meringue (see Karabeej on page 139), it was the most natural thing to try to make halawe (halva) next. Halawe means "sweet" or "sweetness" and is a fudge-like confection. This tahini version is made by making a meringue, setting it with hot sugar syrup, then mixing it with tahini until firm. Halva is commonly sold in supermarkets in plastic packs and can come plain, or studded with pistachios or hazelnuts, or flavoured with cocoa powder. It was my favourite sweet bite to have inside a roll of flatbread during Lent when we couldn't have any dairy. In Saida, you can buy halva by the kilo from special shops that have big blocks to cut from and they generously hand out samples for tasting.

In a large bowl or a stand mixer, beat the soapwort water until fluffy and forming firm peaks.

Combine the sugar and water in a small saucepan over a medium heat and heat until the sugar has dissolved. Add the lemon juice (or citric acid) to prevent crystallisation and continue to heat until the mixture reaches 149°C (300°F) on a sugar thermometer.

Drizzle the hot sugar syrup in a thin stream over the soapwort meringue while beating. Keep mixing until the mixture lowers in temperature.

Add the tahini and salt and mix with a spatula until the texture becomes fluffy and all the tahini and meringue is incorporated.

Leave plain or add the optional add-ins to make a pistachio or hazelnut halva. Pour into a container and leave to cool and set.

Alternatively, dust the sides of a container with a little of the cocoa powder and pour in half of the halva mixture. Mix the remaining cocoa powder into the remaining halva, then pour this into the container over the plain layer. Swirl gently a few times with a spoon or skewer to create a marbled effect. Leave to cool and set.

Will keep for 2–3 months in an airtight container.

MAKES 450 G (1 LB)

75 ml (⅓ cup) soapwort water
(see page 139)

200 g (scant 1 cup) white
granulated sugar

50 ml (¼ cup minus 2 teaspoons) water

1 teaspoon lemon juice
(or ⅛ teaspoon citric acid)

250 g (scant 1 cup) tahini

¼ teaspoon fine salt

35 g (1¼ oz) pistachios or roasted
hazelnuts (optional)

1 tablespoon cocoa powder (optional)

Index

A

aish el saraya x layali loubnan 162
Akkawi 101
    see also Czech Akkawi
akras bil zaytoun 41
al mann w al salwa 199
almonds
    ameh Berbara 184
    ma'arouk 42
    mwara'a 117
    ouze 91
    riz bhalib 180
ameh Berbara 184
aniseeds
    ameh Berbara 184
    aniseed bread for Ramadan 28
    ka'ak asfar 31
    maakroun 174–5
    malateet 141
    Maronite qorban 36
    sfouf 153
    sfouf bi debes 154
    zalabye 45
apples: cocktail fweke she'af 182
Arabic coffee, date & cardamom
    cake 161
arayes msakhan 88
arishe w asal 185
Armenian lahm baajine 56–8
artichokes: rqaqat ardi shawki w
    sbanekh 64
ashta 101, 102
    aish el saraya x layali loubnan 162
    cocktail fweke she'af 182
    hakawet el shmayse 122
    halawet el jeben 124–5
    mafrouke/daoukiye 126
    osmalliye mess 104
    shaabiyat 110
avocado
    cocktail fweke she'af 182
    crispy tuna rice bites 73
awarma (lamb confit)
    fatayer batata 84
    manouchet bayd bi awarma 52
awaymet maa zanjabeel 179

B

bagels: ka'ak al-qods 38
bakeries 7, 15
baklava
    baklawa asabea' 107
    baklawa ballouriye 111
    baklawa borma 114–15
    baklawa taj el malek 108
    burnt Basque baklava
      cheesecake 158
    mwara'a 117
bananas
    arishe w asal 185
    cocktail fweke she'af 182
barazek 147
Basque baklava cheesecake 158
beef
    Armenian lahm baajine 56–8
    borek soujok w jebne 80
    Lebanese lahm baajine 56–8
    muhammara kibbeh 67–9
    ouze 91
    pomegranate molasses lahm
      baajine 56–8
    sambousik lahme/jebne 82
    sfeeha Baalbekiye 74
beetroot (beet)
    mshabbak 173
    whipped feta and beetroot
      tartine toasts 92–3
beignets: tamriye 192
Bilad Al Sham 17
Black Forest cake, Lebanese-style 155
borek soujok w jebne 80
breads & topped breads 18–59
    akras bil zaytoun 41
    arayes msakhan 88
    cheese & pepper paste
      manouche 49
    ka'ak al-qods 38
    ka'ak asfar 13, 21, 31
    lahm baajine 56–8
    ma'arouk 42
    manouchet bayd bi awarma 52
    manouchet harr 55
    manouchet jebne 48
    manouchet shakshouka 54
    manouchet za'atar 46
    Maronite qorban 36
    meshtah Ramadan 28
    qorban 34
    saj 7, 21, 26–7
    taboon 21, 22–5
    tartine toasts 92–3
    zalabye 21, 45

brioche: ma'arouk 42
brittle bars: festiyeh 148
burghul
    kibbet samak 70–1
    muhammara kibbeh 67–9
butter
    burnt Basque baklava
      cheesecake 158
    knefe/knafe nabulsiye 121

C

cakes 131
    aish el saraya x layali loubnan 162
    Arabic coffee, date & cardamom
      cake 161
    burnt Basque baklava
      cheesecake 158
    fôret noire 155
    qizha 156
    sfouf 153
    sfouf bi debes 154
candied pumpkin jam with pumpkin
    spice 189
caramel: Arabic coffee, date &
    cardamom cake 161
cardamom
    al mann w al salwa 199
    Arabic coffee, date & cardamom
      cake 161
carob molasses: sfouf bi debes 154
cashews: baklawa borma 114–15
cheese 101
    arishe w asal 185
    cheese & pepper paste
      manouche 49
    fig jam, mozzarella, walnut and
      honey tartine toasts 92–3
    see also Czech Akkawi, feta cheese
cheesecake
    aish el saraya x layali loubnan 162
    burnt Basque baklava
      cheesecake 158
chicken
    arayes msakhan 88
    fatayer mhammar 87
chillies: akras bil zaytoun 41
chocolate
    fôret noire 155
    ma'arouk 42
    qizha 156
    tarboosh 168
cinnamon: mammouniye 170
cocktail fweke she'af 182
coconut
    ameh Berbara 184
    ma'arouk 42

coffee: Arabic coffee, date &
  cardamom cake 161
cookies 131
  barazek 147
  ghraybe 143
  kaak al Abbas 144
  karabeej maa natef 139–40
  maamoul 131, 132–4
  malateet 141
cornmeal: herby corn crackers 96
cottage cheese, *ashta* 102
crackers for dips 96
cream
  ashta 102
  fôret noire 155
  osmalliye mess 104
  roasted nectarines with orange
    blossom labneh cream, honey
    and pistachios 186
crystal baklava with pistachios 111
cucumber: whipped feta, za'atar,
  tomato, cucumber and lemon
  tartine toasts 92–3
Czech Akkawi 101
  borek soujok w jebne 80
  cheese & pepper paste
    manouche 49
  fatayer zaytoun w jebne 81
  halawet el jeben 124–5
  knefe/knafe nabulsiye 121
  mammouniye 170
  manouchet bayd bi awarma 52
  manouchet jebne 48
  rqaqat ardi shawki w sbanekh 64
  rqaqat jebne 66
  sambousik lahme/jebne 82
  souborek 79

D

dates
  Arabic coffee, date & cardamom
    cake 161
  maamoul 132–4
  ma'arouk 42
doughnuts
  awaymet maa zanjabeel 179
  maakroun 174–5

E

Easter 13
  ka'ak asfar 31
  maamoul 131, 132–4
eggs
  hummus/*muhammara* and spiced
    eggs tartine toasts 92–3
  manouchet bayd bi awarma 52

Eid: *maamoul* 131, 132–4
Epiphany 13
  zalabye 45

F

fatayer 14
  fatayer batata 84
  fatayer mhammar 87
  fatayer zaytoun w jebne 81
festiyeh 148
feta cheese
  sambousik lahme/jebne 82
  souborek 79
  whipped feta and beetroot tartine
    toasts 92–3
  whipped feta, za'atar, tomato,
    cucumber and lemon tartine
    toasts 92–3
fig jam
  fig jam, mozzarella, walnut and
    honey tartine toasts 92–3
  riz bhalib 180
fig leaves: *awaymet maa
  zanjabeel* 179
filo pastry 101
  baklawa asabea' 107
  burnt Basque baklava
    cheesecake 158
  ouze 91
  shaabiyat 110
  souborek 79
fish
  crispy tuna rice bites 73
  fish *kibbeh* 70–1
  kibbet samak 70–1
flatbreads 21
  arayes msakhan 88
  lahm baajine 56–8
  saj 7, 26–7
  taboon 21, 22–5
  tartine toasts 92–3
fôret noire 155
fritters: *mshabbak* 173
fruit
  arishe w asal 185
  cocktail *fweke she'af* 182
  fôret noire 155

G

ghee
  baklawa asabea' 107
  baklawa borma 114–15
  baklawa taj el malek 108
  osmalliye mess 104
ghraybe 143
ginger: *awaymet maa zanjabeel* 179

H

hakawet el shmayse 122
halawe tahiniye 200
halawet el jeben 124–5
halawet el smeed 191
halva: *halawe tahiniye* 200
hand pies
  fatayer mhammar 87
  sambousik lahme/jebne 82
herby corn crackers 96
honey
  al mann w al salwa 199
  cocktail *fweke she'af* 182
  fig jam, mozzarella, walnut and
    honey tartine toasts 92–3
  roasted nectarines with orange
    blossom labneh cream, honey
    and pistachios 186
hummus and spiced eggs tartine
  toasts 92–3

J

jazariye 189
jebne, manouchet 48
Jerusalem sesame bagels 38

K

kaak al Abbas 144
ka'ak al-qods 38
ka'ak asfar 13, 21, 31
karabeej maa natef 139–40
kataifi pastry 101
  baklawa ballouriye 111
  baklawa borma 114–15
  baklawa taj el malek 108
  knefe/knafe nabulsiye 121
  mafrouke/daoukiye 126
  osmalliye mess 104
kibbeh
  kibbet samak 70–1
  muhammara kibbeh 67–9
King's crown baklava 108
knefe/knafe nabulsiye 121

L

labneh
  burnt Basque baklava
    cheesecake 158
  griddled tomato, labneh,
    pomegranate molasses and
    mint tartine toasts 92–3
  roasted nectarines with orange
    blossom labneh cream, honey
    and pistachios 186

rqaqat ardi shawki w sbanekh 64
sambousik lahme/jebne 82
whipped feta and beetroot
  tartine toasts 92–3
whipped feta, za'atar, tomato,
  cucumber and lemon tartine
  toasts 92–3
lahm baajine 56–8
lamb
  ouze 91
  see also awarma
lavender: *mshabbak* 173
Lebanese *lahm baajine* 56–8
Lebanese-style Black Forest cake 155
lemons
  kibbet samak 70–1
  whipped feta, za'atar, tomato,
    cucumber and lemon tartine
    toasts 92–3

M

maakroun 174–5
maamoul 13, 21, 131, 132
ma'arouk 42
mafrouke/daoukiye 126
majdoule 101
malateet 131, 141
mammouniye 170
mango
  cocktail *fweke she'af* 182
  crispy tuna rice bites 73
manouche 7, 14
  cheese & pepper paste
    manouche 49
  manouchet bayd bi awarma 52
  manouchet harr 55
  manouchet jebne 48
  manouchet shakshouka 54
  manouchet za'atar 46
Marie biscuits: *tarboosh* 168
Maronite holy bread buns 36
Maronite *qorban* 36
mayonnaise: crispy tuna rice bites
  73
meringue
  karabeej maa natef 139–40
  tarboosh 168
meshtah Ramadan 28
mhammar hand pies 87
milk
  arishe w asal 185
  ashta 102
  riz bhalib 180
mshabbak 173
mshallale cheese 101
muhammara 67

muhammara and spiced eggs
  tartine toasts 92–3
muhammara kibbeh 67–9
mushrooms: vegan *lahm baajine*
  56–8
mwara'a 117

N

Nabulsi cheese 101
nectarines: roasted nectarines with
  orange blossom labneh cream,
  honey and pistachios 186
nigella seeds: *zalabye* 45
nougat: *al mann w al salwa* 199
nuts
  al mann w al salwa 199
  baklawa borma 114–15
  cocktail *fweke she'af* 182
  jazariye 189
  see also almonds, pine nuts,
    pistachios, walnuts

O

olives
  akras bil zaytoun 41
  fatayer zaytoun w jebne 81
onions
  arayes msakhan 88
  fatayer batata 84
  fatayer mhammar 87
  manouchet harr 55
  manouchet shakshouka 54
orange blossom water
  ashta 102
  baklawa taj el malek 108
  ghraybe 143
  karabeej maa natef 139–40
  knefe/knafe nabulsiye 121
  maamoul 131, 132–4
  Maronite *qorban* 36
  qorban 34
  riz bhalib 180
  roasted nectarines with orange
    blossom labneh cream, honey
    and pistachios 186
  simple syrup 103
Orthodox holy bread 34
osmalliye mess 104
ouze 91

P

Palestinian black cake 156
Palestinian flatbread 21, 22–5
Palestinian sumac chicken and
  onion pitas 88

Palestinian vegan anise cookies
  141
Palestinian yellow Easter bread 31
pastries
  borek soujok w jebne 80
  fatayer batata 84
  fatayer mhammar 87
  fatayer zaytoun w jebne 81
  ouze 91
peanuts: *festiyeh* 148
peas: spiced meat and rice parcels
  91
peppers
  Armenian *lahm baajine* 56–8
  cheese & pepper paste
    manouche 49
  fatayer mhammar 87
  manouchet harr 55
  manouchet shakshouka 54
  muhammara kibbeh 67–9
  sfeeha Baalbekiye 74
  vegan *lahm baajine* 56–8
pies
  borek soujok w jebne 80
  fatayer mhammar 87
  ouze 91
  sambousik lahme/jebne 82
  sfeeha Baalbekiye 74
  souborek 79
pine nuts
  ameh Berbara 184
  baklawa borma 114–15
pistachios
  aish el saraya x layali loubnan
    162
  al mann w al salwa 199
  ameh Berbara 184
  baklawa asabea' 107
  baklawa ballouriye 111
  baklawa borma 114–15
  baklawa taj el malek 108
  barazek 147
  burnt Basque baklava
    cheesecake 158
  ghraybe 143
  karabeej maa natef 139–40
  maamoul 132–4
  mafrouke/daoukiye 126
  mammouniye 170
  osmalliye mess 104
  roasted nectarines with orange
    blossom labneh cream, honey
    and pistachios 186
  shaabiyat 110
pita breads 21
  arayes msakhan 88
  tartine toasts 92–3

pomegranate molasses
    griddled tomato, labneh,
        pomegranate molasses and
        mint tartine toasts 92–3
    lahm baajine 56–8
    muhammara kibbeh 67–9
potatoes
    fatayer batata 84
    fatayer mhammar 87
puff pastry: *fatayer mhammar* 87
pumpkin: *jazariye* 189

Q

qizha 156
qorban 34
    Maronite *qorban* 36

R

raha (lokum) 196
raisins
    ameh Berbara 184
    ma'arouk 42
Ramadan 8
    aniseed bread for Ramadan 28
rice
    crispy tuna rice bites 73
    hakawet el shmayse 122
    ouze 91
    riz bhalib 180
riz bhalib 180
rose jam: *osmalliye* mess 104
rose water
    ashta 102
    baklawa asabea' 107
    baklawa taj el malek 108
    karabeej maa natef 139–40
    maamoul 131, 132–4
    Maronite *qorban* 36
    osmalliye mess 104
    raha (lokum) 196
    riz bhalib 180
    simple syrup 103
rqaqat ardi shawki w sbanekh 64
rqaqat jebne 66

S

saffron: *knefe/knafe nabulsiye* 121
saj 7, 21, 26–7
sambousik lahme/jebne 82
sausages: *borek soujok w jebne* 80
semolina 101
    aish el saraya x layali loubnan 162
    ashta 102
    halawet el jeben 124–5
    halawet el smeed 191

kaak al Abbas 144
karabeej maa natef 139–40
knefe/knafe nabulsiye 121
maakroun 174–5
maamoul 131, 132–4
mammouniye 170
qizha 156
sfouf 153
sfouf bi debes 154
tamriye 192
sesame seeds
    barazek 147
    ka'ak al-qods 38
    ka'ak asfar 31
    ma'arouk 42
    malateet 141
    qizha 156
    sfouf 153
    zalabye 45
sfeeha Baalbekiye 74
sfouf 153
sfouf bi debes 154
shaabiyat 110
shakshouka, manouchet 54
shrimp: *kibbet samak* 70–1
simple syrup 101, 103
    baklawa asabea' 107
    baklawa ballouriye 111
    baklawa borma 114–15
    halawet el jeben 124–5
    osmalliye mess 104
    shaabiyat 110
soapwort water
    al mann w al salwa 199
    halawe tahiniye 200
    karabeej maa natef 139–40
souborek 79
soujok: borek soujok w jebne 80
spiced Abbas cookies 144
spiced fried dough for Epiphany 45
spiced meat and rice parcels 91
spicy flour crackers 96
spicy sausage and cheese pies 80
spinach: *rqaqat ardi shawki w
    sbanekh* 64
spring roll wrappers
    rqaqat ardi shawki w sbanekh 64
    rqaqat jebne 66
strawberries
    arishe w asal 185
    cocktail *fweke she'af* 182
sumac: *arayes msakhan* 88
sweet cheese and semolina rolls with
    ashta, halawet el jeben 124–5
sweet lavender fritters 173
sweet shops 8
sweet stuffed brioche 42

Syrian pistachio and sesame
    cookies 147
Syrian semolina pudding 170

T

taboon 21, 22–5
tahini: *halawe tahiniye* 200
tamriye 192
tannour 21
tarboosh 168
tartine toasts 92–3
tomatoes
    Armenian *lahm baajine* 56–8
    griddled tomato, labneh,
        pomegranate molasses and mint
        tartine toasts 92–3
    Lebanese *lahm baajine* 56–8
    manouchet shakshouka 54
    sfeeha Baalbekiye 74
    vegan *lahm baajine* 56–8
    whipped feta, za'atar, tomato,
        cucumber and lemon tartine
        toasts 92–3
tuna: crispy tuna rice bites 73
Turkish delight 196
turmeric
    ka'ak asfar 31
    turmeric cake, *sfouf* 153

V

vegan *lahm baajine* 56–8

W

wafers: *tarboosh* 168
walnuts
    ameh Berbara 184
    fig jam, mozzarella, walnut and
        honey tartine toasts 92–3
    maamoul 132–4
    muhammara kibbeh 67–9
    mwara'a 117
    riz bhalib 180
wheat grains: *ameh Berbara* 184

Z

za'atar
    manouchet za'atar 46
    whipped feta, za'atar, tomato,
        cucumber and lemon tartine
        toasts 92–3
zalabye 21, 45

Acknowledgements

This book was a real challenge to make, both emotionally and practically. I have talked about things personal to me – the humble refugee neighbourhood and tiny house I grew up and lived in for most of my life – and I have also touched on sensitive topics that the world is finding hard deal with, at a time of warfare in and around my homelands. I worked on the recipes not knowing whether I could be forced to leave Lebanon before I reached the year's end. It crossed my mind that maybe I was writing the recipes for myself, in case I needed to recreate dishes from home in a place far away from it. It was a time of questioning, of trying to make decisions but failing, of wandering aimlessly and not being able to call anywhere or anything "home". At the time of writing, I still have no idea where I might end up – perhaps by the time you're reading this, I may have been uprooted and planted in a different country. Regardless, I would love for this book and these recipes to find a home on your shelves and in your kitchen.

I want to celebrate our culture and speak of our history. Many of the recipes in this book are ones that have been perfected through years of experience by talented bakers and artisans. I have tried to be as detailed as possible in my writing to aid both those who are making them out of curiosity or out of nostalgia for favourite foods that might be out of reach.

The challenges of making this book were made bearable by the support of my family: my mom and dad, my sister, and my chosen family, Charbel and Hanine, who were by my side the whole way, trying out recipes, tasting and suggesting changes. I'm also grateful to my Clown Me In family, whose presence and the work we do together is what helps me remain hopeful during these troubled times.

Lastly, I am thankful to Paul McNally, the publisher at Smith Street Books in Australia, and Emily Preece-Morrison, my publisher and commissioning editor in the UK, who both trusted me with another book and were patient with me throughout all the delays and extensions I requested. And to all those who produced the book, including Georgie Hewitt, Lix and Max Haarala Hamilton, Valerie Berry and Max Robinson – who worked so hard to recreate the recipes and bring them to life.

About the Author

Hisham Assaad is a Lebanese chef, food stylist, graphic designer and photographer who shares recipes and stories on his blog, *cookin5m2*, which focuses on the challenges of cooking good food in a tiny home kitchen in Beirut.

Raised in a food-loving family who were expelled to Lebanon from their village in Palestine in the 1940s, Hisham grew up in Dbayeh, a Palestinian refugee camp on the outskirts of Beirut. He learned about Levantine food by watching his mother (a talented home cook) and father (from a family of butchers) in the kitchen from a young age. They bestowed the basics on him and he took it from there, building a culinary repertoire to satisfy his avid appetite for the food of his homeland. Hisham brings his heritage as part of the Palestinian diaspora to bear on recipes in danger of being lost to history, preserving them for future generations.

He has worked as a guide on boutique food tours of Beirut and the surrounding countryside for *Taste Lebanon* and is a frequent guest chef at local restaurants and festivals. He also works as a humanitarian clown with Clown Me In, a local NGO that seeks to democratise the arts, bringing them to people and going where love and laughter is needed.

His work has been featured in print and online media as well as on television and radio, including a weekly show with a well-known Lebanese host giving culinary tips and recipes since 2020. This is his second book; the first was *Bayrut: The Cookbook*.

Published in 2024 by Smith Street Books
Naarm (Melbourne) | Australia
smithstreetbooks.com

ISBN: 978-1-9230-4943-7

Smith Street Books respectfully acknowledges the Wurundjeri People of the Kulin Nation, who are the Traditional Owners of the land on which we work, and we pay our respects to their Elders past and present.

Publisher: Emily Preece-Morrison
Designer: Georgie Hewitt
Photographers: Haarala Hamilton
Food stylist: Valerie Berry
Prop stylist: Max Robinson
Proofreader: Vicky Orchard
Indexer: Vanessa Bird

Printed & bound in China by C&C Offset Printing Co., Ltd.

Book 343
10 9 8 7 6 5 4 3 2 1

Measurements: This book uses 15 ml tablespoons.

To sterilise glass jars: Wash jars and lids in a dishwasher or plenty of hot, soapy water. Rinse thoroughly, then place upside-down on a baking sheet lined with baking paper and dry for 10 minutes in an oven preheated to 180°C (350°F/gas 4). Handle with care.